# MOORCROFT

Winds of Change

Emma Bossons. 01.01.2000.

Fraser Street

# MOORCROFT

## Winds of Change

WM PUBLICATIONS

First published in 2000 by W M Publications Limited

5 Town Street, Thaxted, Essex CM6 2LD

Distributed by W M Publications Limited

P.O.Box 2864, Ringwood, Hampshire BH24 3YE

Printed in Great Britain by Butler and Tanner, Frome and London

Editor: Ann Geneva

Design: Peter Campbell

Co-ordination: Elise Adams

Photographs: Gate Studios; Gary Leggett Studios; Richard Blower

This book would not have been possible without the help of many people. I must thank,
in particular, Philip Allen, Lynn Cooper, Elliot Hall, Kim Thompson,
Peter Donovan, Ken and Hillie Manley, Rachel Bishop and members of the Moorcroft
Design Studio, Alan Wright, Keith Dawson and, most specially, my best friend,
partner, collaborator, critic, companion and wife, Maureen Edwards.

H.R.E.

Moorcroft Pottery can be found in Cobridge
on Sandbach Road, Stoke-on-Trent ST6 2QD
Telephone: 01782 214 323 Facsimile: 01782 283 455
Moorcroft Collectors' Club Telephone: 01782 820 510

# Contents

TO ALAN WRIGHT,
MASTER SALESMAN – WITH DEEPEST THANKS

# Introduction

'Moorcroft is not about reality, but about stories and dreams.'

*Fraser Street*

The writer Arnold Bennett is usually credited with creating the most telling descriptions of the Potteries, portraying in his stories what he called 'the grim smile of the Five Towns'. His characters have names which seem eerily familiar to anyone associated with Moorcroft – Emery, Penkethman, Slaney and others. One of Bennett's most evocative portraits of the five towns which make up Stoke on Trent enables the reader almost to smell and taste the soot-filled air and hear the roar of the bottle kilns as they fire fine wares for the delectation of the civilised world:

> the singular scenery of coal dust, potshards, flame and steam... It was squalid ugliness, but it was squalid ugliness on a scale so vast and overpowering that it became sublime. Great furnaces gleamed red in the twilight, and their fires were reflected in horrible black canals; processions of heavy vapour drifted in all directions across the sky, over what acres of mean and miserable brown architecture! The air was alive with the most extraordinary, weird, gigantic sounds. I do not think the Five Towns will ever be described: Dante lived too soon!

It is hard to imagine a greater contrast – either between the inferno of its origins in Bennett's day and the fine china set upon the table by ladies (or their maids) or between the Potteries of Bennett's description and the light and lustre of today's Moorcroft Works.

And yet, while nowhere near matching Bennett's industrial squalor, the deadening atmosphere of failure which hung over the company in 1986, when Hugh Edwards and his partners took over Moorcroft under a dramatic 24-hour deadline, was grim enough. Reduced to a staff of 14 from its heyday in the 1920s, with sales even in the London area having dwindled to a pittance, the company which had boasted a proud tradition since 1913 was on its knees.

The founder of Moorcroft pottery William Moorcroft had been born in 1872 in Burslem, Staffordshire, where his namesake Works is still located today. His family was already linked to the Potteries, since his father Thomas was a well-known designer and china painter who specialised in floral decoration. By 1895 William was studying pottery and porcelain in the collections of London's Museums, while attending what later became the Royal College of Art. William's career as a potter was launched when at the age of 24 he was offered a position as a designer with the china and earthenware manufacturers James Macintyre & Company in Burslem. Macintyre had diversified in 1893 into producing the ornamental art pottery made popular by William Morris and his followers. In March 1897 William Moorcroft took up his post, immediately designing new shapes and introducing an original stylised floral decoration.

William Moorcroft drew his designs 'in the round', adapting them to fit every shape of pot. Rare for a potter and designer William had made a study of ceramic chemistry, which provided him with an understanding of the firm's laboratories, clayrooms, and dipping house, as well as the kilns in which the ware was fired. His knowledge of the entire spectrum of pottery design and manufacture enabled him to originate and supervise the whole range of ceramic production.

In 1898 William developed a new range of decorative pottery using techniques of slip-trailing and underglaze colour, which were to become his hallmarks. The result was called Florian ware, reflecting the floral basis of its motifs, which proved a great and immediate success. Within a year of being introduced, Florian ware was on sale at Liberty of London and Rouard of Paris, as well as Tiffany in New York. During the period he worked for Macintyre, William's name gained international recognition. At the same age as Moorcroft designer Rachel Bishop was awarded her first gold medal, William won his at the St. Louis International Exhibition of 1904. He eventually became the first person to register his name as a Trademark.

When in 1912 William Moorcroft was told by Macintyre that it was to cease producing ornamental pottery, he turned to Liberty for financial backing to build a new factory in which he could continue to produce his distinctive ware. With Liberty providing most of the finances, a new state-of-the-art factory arose in 1913 on the site of a former tile and brick company in Cobridge, where Moorcroft remains to this day. There William moved his team of 34 craftsmen and women, all of whom had worked with him at Macintyre. William's greatest technical achievement was the low temperature soft flambé glazes he was able to perfect after building a special flambé kiln in 1919. Central to Moorcroft's growing world-wide modishness was the patronage extended by the royal family, and especially Queen Mary.

In 1928 Moorcroft Pottery was granted a Royal Warrant, and it continued to be honoured with awards. Even the fascist dictator Benito Mussolini became an avid collector after William won a medal in Milan in 1933. The Depression and World War II took a great toll on William, who pushed both his factory and his own spirit to the limit. In 1945 he was taken ill and survived only long enough for his elder son Walter to arrive home on compassionate leave from the army.

Walter, who inherited artistic flair, had begun working with his father in 1935 directly from school. William passed on to Walter not only his working methods, but also insights into every aspect of pottery design and manufacture – including his fiercely guarded flambé methods. After Walter assumed command of the company he sustained design as well as the company's reputation until his retirement in 1987. Perhaps more importantly, Walter greatly reduced the hazards and improved the conditions under which the Moorcroft staff worked. John Moorcroft, William's younger son from his second marriage to Hazel Lasenby of the Liberty family, joined the company in 1962 with special responsibility for sales. John has continued as roving ambassador for his family name.

By the time of his death, examples of Moorcroft's work had been acquired by museums around the world, culminating in 1972 when the Victoria and Albert Museum mounted a retrospective centenary exhibition of William's design work. Throughout his lengthy career, William Moorcroft never employed a manager or another designer, insisting on responsibility for every aspect of production. He once styled himself, 'Potter, Chemist, Designer, Managing Director, Secretary' – a combination no one person could ever again embody.

By 1986, however, Europe's last family-owned art pottery had not created a major new design for fifteen years. In *Moorcroft – the Phoenix Years*, Fraser Street – with his uniquely close vantage point to Hugh Edwards – revealed the inside story of the dramatic revival of England's best-loved art pottery. For Fraser Street life is a vast stage, and he peopled his vivid drama with an unforgettable cast of characters.

There was irascible colour alchemist and Works Manager Justin Emery; bow-tied sales saviour Alan Wright; eagle-eyed editor Maureen Edwards; dapper

Mr John and wise-cracking Gill; and, of course, design prodigy Rachel Bishop, who at the age of 24 was only the fourth Moorcroft designer in its almost-100-year history. Together they and the growing workforce accomplished the impossible, and Moorcroft went from strength to strength.

Now the phoenix which rose from the ashes finds himself being borne along on the winds of change.

*Ann Geneva*

MOORCROFT: WINDS OF CHANGE

ABOVE: Steven, Rachel and Alan at the centenary party, January 1, 1997.
BELOW: Thaxted Morris Men celebrate the Moorcroft centenary at midnight

# ONE

# Phoenix Crash Lands

It was a clear winter's night and a light wind blew gently over the East Anglian plains carrying with it that unmistakable iron cold of the Siberian mountains. The lights had been switched on in Thaxted church to invite all those who passed by to come inside and see in the new year. From the Swan Hotel immediately opposite could be heard the cheerful buzz of conversation between friends, punctuated by the occasional outburst of laughter. Maureen Edwards was sharing a private joke or two with Thaxted people who had done so much to support her husband Hugh after he stood down as chairman of Thaxted Council more than ten years earlier to immerse himself in Moorcroft Pottery. Neville Pundole, Kim Thompson and her husband Chris were talking together with Debbie Edwards by a log fire at the far end of the room. Alan Wright and Steven Swann were looking intently at a small wood engraving of the Works which Moorcroft designer, Rachel Bishop, was holding. Steven would have travelled down from Stoke on Trent with the Thompsons that day, but Hugh Edwards had no idea where Rachel's journey had started. Graham Soal and his wife Margaret sat together. After Hugh and Maureen had joined Moorcroft back in 1986, it had been Graham, as their personal bank manager, who had first approved the availability of funds to invest in the company. In those days, Moorcroft had been in dire financial straits. Everyone in the room had played a part in Moorcroft's recovery and all deserved a personal vote of thanks. At five minutes to midnight, Hugh unobtrusively left the hotel with his wife to walk across to Thaxted church. Others followed him, including Rachel and the Wrights. He was conscious of that. The Thaxted Morris Men were already inside the church, dancing to the sound of a traditional tune, each holding a 31cm Moorcroft Snakeshead vase. The great church clock struck midnight. Simultaneously, the Thaxted bells pealed their message of joy at the arrival of the new year across the open countryside. It was

1997, and the first pots to carry the Moorcroft name were one hundred years old.

An hour later, with the sound of the Thaxted Morris Men still pounding in their ears, the Edwards walked back to the Swan Hotel. Moorcroft designer, Rachel Bishop, had taken up the rope of one of the great church bells to help the Thaxted band of ringers welcome in the new year with a peal of bells. American journalist, Ann Geneva, and Rachel's father, Martin, took up others. It required considerable strength, Hugh thought to himself, to pull the great bell ropes and considerable courage to dance holding 31cm Moorcroft pots. The sight of the Thaxted Morris Men swinging their grey, black and maroon Snakeshead vases in great circles above their heads was something all of those present were unlikely to forget, not least the Morris Men themselves, who seemed tense, even nervous. Yet for some inexplicable reason Hugh felt a crushing sense of anticlimax. Instead of exhilaration at the arrival of Moorcroft's centenary, the reality was altogether different. Inside he felt empty; his enthusiasm had drained away, something that had never happened before. The winds of emotion and vision which always brought joy and happiness throughout his life had simply died away. As people offered genuine and warm congratulations, Hugh felt as if they were offering them to someone else. It was as if he had ceased to exist.

Still detached, and with 1997 less than a month old, Hugh watched sales of Moorcroft's Centenary Carousel surge forward. The phenomenal success of the brilliantly coloured Carousel charger was especially rewarding, carrying as it did examples of many of the design themes used by Moorcroft designers over the preceding hundred years. Moorcroft designer, Rachel Bishop, had worked hard to bring forward designs of great beauty to celebrate Moorcroft's centenary, but what would have happened to Moorcroft if she had fallen ill during the creative process of design? What would Moorcroft then have been able to offer its collectors for the greatest celebration in its corporate life? In reality, Rachel had done more than could have been reasonably expected of her, but the vulnerability of an art pottery relying solely on a single person was a thought which recurred time and time again.

Quite early in the new year a very real problem reared its head. William Moorcroft's Yacht vase, designed almost a century earlier, began to show the first signs of a design fault that was to become more critical as the weeks passed by. A dark blue collar on the neck of the vase literally dripped when the glaze was in a molten state in the kiln, speckling its wide base with the occasional blue spot. This design fault was enough to cause seven out of eight vases to be designated as 'seconds'. Happily, if William Moorcroft's original design had been flawed, his elder son, Walter, had surpassed himself. For Walter Moorcroft, his landscape After the Storm was a revolutionary design, and all two hundred pieces in the edition were sold before the end of February.

Best wishes poured into the Moorcroft Works from all over the world; but despite the praise, Hugh found himself unable to anchor his thoughts or see a clear way forward. Somehow he had lost his inspiration, his ability to dream and plan his way into the future. Only a month after leaving behind good friends and partners at his old law firm, Richards Butler, he had begun to miss them badly. Sometimes Stoke on Trent seemed far away, a lonely, alien place, full of alien people with an alien culture. More than once Hugh found himself worrying about the possibility that despite twelve long years dedication to Moorcroft already, he would never be able to transplant himself fully into a new life and work for the company virtually full time, guiding it from its centenary into the new millennium.

Throughout the cold winter months of 1997, Hugh's own very personal crisis intensified. Only the warmth and support from Maureen, his wife of more than thirty-two years standing, and his four children, kept mind and soul together. This was not how it was meant to be. In all his calculations he had underestimated the emotional effect of dismantling, brick by brick, the wall of his legal career. Retire at the top and go to Moorcroft, his friends had said. Little did they know what this meant in practice.

Matters were made worse by the emptiness of Moorcroft's two-up, two-down miner's cottage in Stoke on Trent, which had doubled for eight years as both a design studio and a transient home for Hugh and his wife, as well as the pottery's occasional visitors. On his first overnight visit to Stoke on Trent, and before the centenary year was more than a few days old, all Hugh could focus on in the little house was the detritus of centenary designs: old drawings and tracings, miscellaneous tube-lined pots, vases partially drawn on which Rachel had abandoned. In the run up to the Centenary, her output had been prodigious by any definition, and there was no obvious reason why one particular design had been preferred to another. For all Hugh knew, there might well be sufficient surplus design ideas just lying around gathering dust to satisfy Moorcroft's design needs for some time to come.

His wife advised him to ignore the muddle or set to and clear it up. The house itself was terraced and sited towards the end of a cul-de-sac tucked unobtrusively under the man-made hill which started life as the slag heap for Cobridge's Sneyd colliery. The hill was covered with stunted trees and wiry grass. When the wind blew, waste paper from surrounding streets would spin in spirals before collapsing outside the front door. This was Cobridge, and Cobridge was a desolate place, particularly in winter. Many of the rows of terraced cottages with their red brick walls and grey slate roofs had been demolished in the name of progress. Some had survived, but in place of those that had been cleared away, a hard-pressed city council had authorised the construction of 'sheds', a developers' euphemism for steel-framed, coloured plastic monstrosities which served as distribution depots or second grade workshops without real light or air. Stoke on Trent's great legacy of bottle ovens had mostly disappeared. So too had the city's industrial heritage of steel and coal. The jobs that went with them had gone as well.

In the evening, sitting alone in that little house, Hugh had plenty of time to contemplate the industrial images of a bygone age in Cobridge. Moorcroft Pottery was still there, its magnificent bottle oven hugging the skyline as if it had been in place forever. At least the bottle oven was real, strong, beautiful, dignified. At the end of the day that was more than could be said of the marble and glass building called Beaufort House, home of the City law firm in London which Hugh had abandoned before Christmas. Simply by comparing the two, Hugh started to think positively. Avoid negative thoughts, his wife and children had told him time and time again.

Gradually his family worked their magic, and Hugh Edwards, the ex-lawyer, found himself regaining control of his own spirit. The old enthusiasm started to return, too. There was the millennium to think about, production capacity to improve to satisfy an ever-growing demand for Moorcroft pottery from collectors all over the world; new jobs to create in that man-made wilderness called Cobridge, and a new Labour government to provide a framework within which he could work. All of this spelt the beginning of a new life. Hugh was ready to embrace it and start serving the Moorcroft workforce. If they committed their lives to England's best-loved art pottery, it was his duty to commit the remainder of his working life to them.

Before the end of January, Hugh mentioned the unmentionable to Rachel. Design responsibilities during 1996 had imposed unacceptable burdens on her, and support was needed. The two of them talked about a kind of human triangle. One corner would be the designer, the second Hugh himself and the third,

Rachel suggested, a person to help the designer with her work. More specifical-ly, what she had in mind was to recruit a person who could learn the arts of both tube-lining and decoration, someone who would act as her junior and work with her in the design studio.

That was not exactly what Hugh had in mind, but at that particular moment he had no positive thoughts in his mind at all. Rachel's argument was persuasive. In theory, a dual-skilled tube-liner and decorator would take the design process out of the Works Manager's conflict zone in the Moorcroft decorating shop – the situation which had so frustrated both Rachel and her predecessor. That frustra-tion had, Rachel said solemnly, sapped her creative energy. The reasoning be-hind her proposal was that design experimentation would be taken away from the Works Manager and into the design studio. In so doing, the great production god would be appeased. No longer would the Works Manager's production schedules be sacrificed for the creative needs of a designer.

Many works managers throughout the Potteries dislike designers as a breed, and Moorcroft's Justin Emery was a man of firm views. A brilliant glaze and colour expert and a more than competent mathematician, he sometimes saw de-signers as an added burden, people who destroyed logic in the otherwise order-ly process of manufacturing objects. In fact, Hugh had noticed this phenomenon several years earlier, but the implications had then been totally lost on him. The reason was simple. The left-brained city man which Hugh used to be had no real understanding of an artist's needs, whether they designed or painted pots. The right-brained, more artistic part of his personality, which in days gone by had even inspired him to write reasonable poetry, had long since become buried under a pile of pretentious legal paper; this in turn had come to represent the sum total of his life's work as a lawyer. To succeed working at Moorcroft full time, he had to learn the precise moment to switch from the left-brained, logical thought processes used by works managers to the right-brained, more artistic qualities of the majority of the workforce, including designers. Most important of all, he had to learn fast.

In what seemed like no time at all, Nicki Lee had joined Rachel at the Works. With the help of Moorcroft's leading decorators and tube-liners, she started to learn Moorcroft's art of decorating and tube-lining, set as a precondition to her full-time employment in the company. To succeed, Nicki had to prove her com-petence in both skills, a tough target by any standard. The effect of her arrival on Rachel was almost instantaneous. Out of the design studio drawers, off shelves

*1997 Moorcroft centennial stand and below the 1924 stand at the Wembley Exhibition*

gathering dust, and even off the top of the resident fridge, came a varied assortment of pots and plates. Rachel Bishop gave every appearance of being a designer about to enter inspiration mode.

By February, the sales team had orchestrated the construction of a new centennial stand for Moorcroft at Birmingham's International Spring Fair at the National Exhibition Centre. Based on original drawings by the same architect who had designed the Moorcroft stand at the great Wembley Exhibition in 1924, the stand builders created an plausible replica. Admittedly the 1997 model was a metre shorter than the original because of fire regulations, but the overall effect of architect Edward Maufe's work was dramatic. Curiously, only when he saw the pots on show did Hugh recognise a potential weakness in Moorcroft's centennial presentation. Apart from a token presence in the Carousel design, fruit had disappeared from the Moorcroft agenda. So too had fish. Both the Carp and Finches Blue designs had been discontinued in 1996 to make way for the centenary pieces.

John Moorcroft had also noticed the weakness, and it had been John, younger son of William Moorcroft, the founding father of the company, who asked Rachel to consider fruit as a design objective for 1998. 'Mr John', as he prefers to be known at the Works, is the high priest of things traditional, and in Mr John's view, Moorcroft needed fruit to support its traditional image. Hugh had not been reticent in putting forward ideas of his own to the Moorcroft designer. Frangipani to replace Magnolia Ivory; Tulip Trees as a design challenge; and some vague ideas on fish to replace Moorcroft's Carp design. In the end nothing came of it, and Hugh decided to leave Rachel alone to seek her own inspiration elsewhere, rather than force issues of his own creation and apply pressure for new designs. Rachel would come back to him with ideas when she was ready.

The first centenary 'in-store' promotion had been fixed for Thursday, 20 March, with Liberty, the prestigious London retailer and one-time owner of Moorcroft stock, acting as host. In reality, the event surreptitiously mutated into Moorcroft's launch of its centennial celebrations, as well as the launch of Fraser Street's book, Moorcroft – the Phoenix Years. The celebrations were orchestrated by the head of Liberty's china and glass department, Julia Marsh. Efficient, intelligent and totally committed to Moorcroft, Julia had planned the day down to the last detail. Moorcroft's sales guru in London and the South East, Alan Wright, had a great respect for her and her strength of purpose in the Moorcroft cause. Julia understood the essence of Moorcroft, the mysterious spirit of the pottery which attached itself to people, seducing them to embrace its beauty and timeless form.

By the time 20 March arrived, more than two thousand copies of *The Phoenix Years* had already been sold, with the designer's father, Martin Bishop, acting as book distributor from his home deep in the New Forest. All the Moorcroft big guns were scheduled to appear at Liberty. That had been Julia Marsh's idea. Walter Moorcroft and Rachel as designers, Hugh as author and Mr John to sign his father's Yacht vase.

To say that the day was a success would be a serious understatement. Collectors queued long before Liberty opened their doors at 9.00 in the morning, and from then on the china and glass department was a never-ending scene of good-humoured turmoil. Witty and gracious at the age of eighty, Walter Moorcroft had a continuous queue of collectors at his table. Knowing of his forty-seven years service to the company, collectors showed their enthusiasm in full measure. Rachel had a smile for everyone. This was not a private celebration. Moorcroft's collecting public came in large numbers to show their appreciation. Hugh found it hard to believe that more than three hundred people actually wanted to buy Phoenix Bird vases and two hundred copies of Fraser Street's book in a single afternoon. Yet however many times he rubbed his eyes, the lines of people standing behind the Moorcroft designer and himself just seemed to grow and grow.

Hugh Edwards' first two months at the Works were not easy. Sometimes he would find himself revisiting his decision to abandon the law, questioning whether or not it had been a mistake. Demands were still being made on him by his former firm. A ten-day tour of the Middle East pencilled in for May bore witness to that. At other times, the avalanche of increasing orders from enthusiastic retailers, and the inability of Moorcroft's artists to cope with them all, raised a different kind of doubt in his mind. There were issues

ABOVE: *Trevor Critchlow craftsman modeller and mould-maker. Mr John looks on.* BELOW: *Alan Wright, master salesman*

*Moorcroft Works, Sandbach Road at the dawn of the centenary year*

of commitment in the wind, one of which crystalised on 21 January when Gill Moorcroft resigned as Collectors' Club Secretary. Gill's rumbustious presence at the Works would be missed. The centenary would bring in its wake the need for a dedicated effort to involve collectors in Moorcroft's centennial celebrations all over the world. The position of Collectors' Club Secretary was not a sinecure based on patronage. It was a job that required hard work, a meticulous eye for detail, and a full understanding of collectors, both young and old. Gill had been with the company since the early 1970s, and it was important to ensure that her departure was not bad for morale. Her successor had to be cheerful, always available, and totally dedicated to Moorcroft, its retailers and collectors alike.

Lady Luck smiled as she occasionally does when a crisis rears its head, and the Moorcroft Board quickly appointed Maggie Williams as replacement Collectors' Club Secretary. Coming from a museum background augured well, and Maggie soon settled down to her task to organise and administer. Hugh had calculated that during the centenary year it was likely that club membership would approximately double. Certainly that was his personal ambition. For Maggie, although only a few months separated her from her sixtieth birthday, there would be much to do. Both Hugh and his colleagues at Moorcroft kept their fingers firmly crossed in the hope that she would be able to cope.

Not surprisingly, to run an art pottery is mainly about the serious business of making and selling pots. Selling the centenary designs was not a problem. Making them was something altogether different. At times Hugh felt that Works Manager Justin Emery was a latter-day King Canute. With the tide of demand for Moorcroft forever advancing, Justin often seemed to sit back, telling it to go away. A production increase of thirty per cent on turnover was not an unrealistic projection for the centenary year, something Hugh had mentioned to Justin on a number of occasions over the previous two years. Despite these reminders, Justin's increase in production failed to come anywhere near the required level. Incoming orders leapt by sixty per cent before the centenary year was three months old, twice as much as even Hugh had forecast, so who was he to criticise?

Given that it takes upwards of a year to train a Moorcroft decorator or tube-liner, the production problems were likely to take a long time to solve, even if the

Works Manager had the will to solve them. Hugh hoped that he had. Still shaken by his own change of career, the Moorcroft Chairman felt empathy with the stress of others. He suspected that Justin, like himself, was stressed. In Hugh's case it was slightly different. His ability to function properly as a manager of people had been seriously weakened by his change in working environment, and his personal task was to ensure that he recovered, adapted his old skills and then applied them for Moorcroft's benefit. Easy in theory; hard in practice, Hugh had commented to his wife.

By the end of March, Steven Swann, the Moorcroft salesman for the north of England, and Alan Wright, Hugh's old friend who looked after the south of England, had nothing to sell. As much pottery as Moorcroft could make in a year or even more had already been sold. This was in stark contrast to the bleak years of 1987 and 1988, when Alan Wright joined Moorcroft and single-handedly opened up London and after that the whole of southern England in a virtuoso sales campaign the like of which even hardened retailers had never seen before. The memory of their first real conversation together in Bethlehem as the two of them sat on what is said to be the manger, was still fresh in Hugh's mind. Alan and Hugh had first met in Jerusalem a day or so earlier – a meeting which Hugh would never forget. Sometimes life brings people together in strange ways, but often for a purpose.

Hugh jokingly told Alan and Steven that they were fired, only to be immediately re-appointed as sales managers with sole responsibility for keeping Moorcroft's retail partners happy. The worry about how best to underpin both Maggie and Rachel was on-going. There was always the possibility that Nicki Lee would fail in either art of tube-lining or decoration. As for the Collectors' Club, it was still early days, but if membership doubled in the centenary year as Hugh had forecast, there was a better than even chance that Maggie Williams would need support too.

Much like the pots that it makes, Moorcroft's own corporate shape was important. After only three months working full time in Stoke on Trent, Hugh had already concluded that Moorcroft was shaped too much like a pole. With such a narrow base it was worryingly vulnerable to changes in fashion or collecting habits. Before Hugh's involvement in the company, a collapse had almost come about both in 1984 and 1986 and only just averted both times. Moorcroft's corporate shape had to be changed if the company was to survive long term, and that meant turning the shape of the company from a pole into a pyramid. Corporate

*Rachel Bishop and camera crew in Australia*

acquisitions and the creation of new businesses both had to be considered. With a three-week tour of Australia and New Zealand scheduled to start at the end of March, Hugh seriously doubted whether he had either the time or mental capacity to handle the tour. Rachel was to go with him to introduce herself to Moorcroft's Antipodean collectors and media with her Phoenix Bird vase. Hugh would take his *Phoenix Years* book.

Two centennial exhibitions had been planned. The first 'Moorcroft – A Century of Colour' was scheduled to open at Saffron Walden Museum on 22 March, while 'Moorcroft – A Hundred Years of a Living Art Pottery' was planned for October at Stoke on Trent's City Museum and Art Gallery, now known as the Potteries Museum and Art Gallery. Hugh and Maureen helped organise both, travelling up and down the British Isles, coaxing and cajoling collectors into lending their treasures for exhibition. The Liberty launch of the centennial celebrations and the Saffron Walden exhibition dates almost coincided.

The Saffron Walden exhibition made a strong start with a record number of visitors attending. A year later, the museum, the oldest purpose-built museum in the United Kingdom (after the British Museum), won the Museum of the Year award for the first time. Whether the exhibition of Moorcroft pots had helped, no one would ever know. It was too soon to start worrying about the Stoke on Trent show. In an ideal world Hugh would have liked to bring forward something dramatic for Stoke on Trent, but final plans would have to wait until his return.

Overseas tours can be tiring as anyone who travels abroad as part of their work or for holidays will readily appreciate. Going in and out of hotels, airport lounges and taxis is tedious. If you add to this television, radio and press commitments in any shape or form, a higher level of attention, concentration and self-awareness is often required.

Despite the pressure, in everything that she did, the Moorcroft designer kept on smiling, talked to Moorcroft collectors, engaged the media with the Moorcroft story and generally acted as a natural and genuine ambassador for the company. Only on the last day in Australia was there cause for real concern. After a long day in Sydney's 'Jewel of Art' store, Rachel slept in the back of the car clearly unwell. Back at the Ritz Carlton hotel, and with increasing alarm, Hugh watched Rachel's breathing depress and her eyes close. At first he thought she was falling asleep. Only when slight convulsions started did he realise that something was seriously wrong.

That night Rachel remained in Sydney's St Vincent's hospital. Hugh never saw her again before the two of them started the long journey home. He travelled alone to New Zealand the following day, telling collectors why the designer was unable to come with him. Messages of regret and best wishes arrived continuously, but with each one Hugh experienced a hollow feeling. This was not how the great Centenary celebrations were meant to turn out. Throughout the Antipodean tour, he had carried a small Hoya vase which Rachel had designed specifically to use for media purposes. For Hugh the vase somehow became a symbol of everything that had gone wrong. The piece would never go into production. That decision was easy.

*Hoya. Height 12 cm (5″).*

*Carp vase*

# TWO

# Collectors Carping

The two of them had arrived at the garden gate of a small thatched cottage in the village of Ashdon in Essex. Hugh and Maureen stood looking at the blue front door for a few moments before walking up the garden path to announce their arrival. It had been a chance phone call, one of those calls which seemed totally inconsequential at the time, but which in some mysterious way gathered significance as the minutes ticked by. The caller was a local school teacher who planned to move house.

From his late mother the teacher had inherited two pieces of Moorcroft pottery. One, a small piece of Pomegranate, had remained almost unnoticed on a window sill for several decades. The other had suffered a more ignominious fate. To prevent dust from percolating into the piece, the school teacher's mother had stuffed a cork into the narrow neck of the vase. Neither vase had been washed for years, and both were coated with a thin film of grease on which the dust of decades had come happily to rest. Nobody knew where the Pomegranate vase had come from, but Edwards judged the piece to be at least ten years younger than its more dramatic and exciting corked companion.

The owner of the vases had been to the Saffron Walden Museum's exhibition, 'Moorcroft – A Century of Colour'. The show had enabled him to identify both pieces. It had also made him realise that the corked vase was a very special vase indeed. The colours were those of William Moorcroft's brown Cornflower design. The shape was that of a double gourd, and like the 'blue on blue' Florian vase in the Saffron Walden exhibition, it carried the famous William Moorcroft Florian carp design.

As he gazed at the corked vase and its decades of grime, the implications of the discovery percolated into the inner reaches of Hugh's collector's brain causing his stomach to churn as never before. The call had not been a dealer's call. It was a call from a retired professional man who had inherited a fine piece of Moorcroft given to his mother on her wedding day in 1913. This corked vase was the Moorcroft find of the decade, if not more. God and its owner willing, the piece could also act as a dramatic focal point for the Stoke on Trent City Museum and Art Gallery's October exhibition, 'Moorcroft – a Hundred Years of a Living Art Pottery'. Hugh had to stop dreaming and regain his composure. As things stood, the vase belonged to a total stranger.

The reality of the piece was better than an optimistic collector's most ambitious expectations. For Hugh, a man who never had expectations about anything, the implication of the discovery was astonishing. Gingerly he removed the vase from its resting place of eighty-four years, a handsome oak desk of considerable antiquity. Then it was washed with a gentle detergent and warm water. As the grime melted away, lovely soft reds, yellows and greens began to shine brightly through the glaze in the form of swimming fish and drifting reeds. The quality was unbelievably fine. As a piece of Moorcroft, it was the most important vase Hugh had ever stumbled upon in the whole of his collecting life. It was also totally different to any other piece of Moorcroft Hugh had ever seen. Before him was a design unquestionably executed by William Moorcroft in the first year or two of the twentieth century, yet for some mysterious reason more than a decade had elapsed before the Ashdon carp vase had been decorated in its own special colourway shortly before the outbreak of the First World War.

No, Hugh told the surprised owner, the Edwards would not buy it. If they did so, the owner would always wonder whether the price paid had been fair. Hugh knew that the piece was worth a five-figure sum, but the best he felt able to do was phone one of the country's leading Moorcroft collectors to see if he was interested in making an offer. If the truth were known, Hugh was surprised that the present owner was prepared to sell the vase at all now that he knew how rare it was. If the Edwards had owned it, the piece would have been harder to prise away than their own teeth!

The phone call was made, and three hours later the Moorcroft collector arrived at the Ashdon cottage. Less than an hour after that, the exquisite double gourd carp vase was travelling to a new home. Before making the introduction Hugh had struck a solitary bargain with the collector. If the purchase was made, the carp vase would be made available for the Stoke on Trent exhibition as the star exhibit for the duration of the show. It was a condition with which the collector happily complied.

Only days after their return from Australia, James Macintyre and Co, leading Moorcroft retailers in Leeds, were scheduled to host the first in-store book promotion after Liberty with Hugh and Rachel in attendance. Hugh doubted that the Moorcroft designer would have recovered from her illness enough to attend, and braced himself for that probability. The shop was run by his daughter Debbie, a full-time dental student at Leeds University. The magnificent Grade I listed Victoria Quarter in Leeds city centre was a superb location for any store and always a pleasure to visit. Macintyre's rubbed shoulders with Harvey Nichols, Vivienne Westwood and many other famous brand names in the picturesque County Arcade.

*Moorcroft Retailer, James Macintyre & Co, Victoria Quarter, Leeds. Debbie Edwards (right) and Elizabeth Haldane.*

In his heart, Hugh knew that collectors would come to the event in large numbers, but many would be disappointed if Rachel failed to turn up, not least of all his own daughter. He was wrong to have doubts! The designer arrived. 'Just for you,' she quipped at Hugh, but it was what the collectors wanted and they showed it in their enthusiasm to meet her. The designer was ready to enjoy the fruits of her success, and little did anyone anticipate what a huge success it would turn out to be. While her designs broke all Moorcroft sales records, Rachel's Phoenix Bird vase, available at all in-store book promotion events, was already set to be the best selling Moorcroft vase of all time.

Towards the end of 1996 the Board decided that the time had come to underpin Justin Emery's efforts as Works Manager by appointing a production manager with special responsibility for training new tube-liners and decorators in Moorcroft's art. The subsequent interviews early in the new year were taken very seriously indeed. A manager who had helped set up Royal Doulton's Indonesian factory was favoured by Hugh. For entirely different and very personal reasons, he also quizzed with interest another applicant, Robert Watson, an artist-potter, chemist, sometime manager and free spirit. Mr John favoured all the applicants one by one, while Maureen considered an applicant by the name of Keith Dawson to be the most able. He was, Hugh pointed out sourly to his wife, wearing a tie but not a jacket.

*Keith Dawson and tube-liner*
*Ailie Woodhead-Coates*

Over the next week, second interviews were planned. Maureen applied awesome pressure on her husband to promote Keith Dawson's cause. A divided husband/wife vote at the second interview would have been unfortunate. Keith Dawson, Maureen insisted, had management instincts closer to Hugh's than any of the other applicants. She had also found out that Keith's brother, Neil, ran the political office of the Member of Parliament for Stoke North, Joan Walley. Stoke North constituency included the Moorcroft factory in Sandbach Road. The deciding factor for her, Maureen told her husband, was that Keith Dawson had left a much earlier employer on grounds of conscience when the company concerned had removed the skull and crossbones emblem from drums of noxious chemicals to 'reassure' employees that they were safe to handle. Maureen won, and Keith Dawson was appointed production manager at Moorcroft.

His battle on behalf of the lady from Royal Doulton lost, Hugh focused his attention once more on Moorcroft's stability as a company, and the inherent weakness of its corporate structure. Without changes in that structure, there was always a chance Moorcroft might start travelling down the slippery road towards extinction once more. That was his perennial problem. While others were grappling with the issues of the present, often identified or created by Hugh in the first place, the man himself was already on a foray into the future. To start the move towards stability and security, something new and dramatic was needed, something which needed a free spirit, a buccaneering instinct and sheer, bloody-minded determination to solve technical problems. Hugh confided in Works Manager Justin Emery that he had not forgotten Robert Watson, another interviewee in the quest for a production manager. The germ of an idea had begun to form around the quite separate skills of Robert Watson and Justin Emery.

Keith's arrival at Sandbach Road was a catalyst to change. When Justin said something could not be done, Keith contrived to do it without upsetting Justin. Recruiting of new staff in the decorating shop started almost immediately and training programmes intensified. Rachel designed a large number of special training pieces, starting with simple, straight forward drawings with more complex designs available as each trainee became more competent. To ensure that training pieces were separately identified from mainstream work, each carried a special 'T' mark on the base. Everyone liked the new training designs and their multiple colourways, and many of those who saw them were quietly seduced into starting mini-collections, so good was the quality of many of them. The 'T' stands for 'Training', of course, even though a few dishonest dealers in the secondary market still attempt to sell them on at a profit by fraudulently representing that the 'T' stands for 'Test market' or 'Trial'.

Before long the Works were full. There was simply no room to seat another decorator, tube-liner or indeed anyone else at all in the building. The recruitment of trainees ground to an abrupt halt. Justin resisted the temptation to indulge in triumphancy. That was not in his nature. The Works Manager's expertise was in colour and glazes, and like his love of mathematics, these skills were inborn, handed down in his family over generations. For the present, Keith lacked a number of Justin's special skills, but he was wise enough to acknowledge the fact and avoid friction. That said, the production manager had special skills of his own. Keith's years with Pilkington Tiles had been good years. Pilkington were fine, honourable employers, and when he left them to join Moorcroft, they paid for a weekend at a top hotel for Keith and his wife, Yvonne. The message was not lost on his new colleagues at Moorcroft. Pilkington would take Keith back at any time, and his special skills had been learned in the manufacture of tiles!

Hugh's own spirits continued to rise, and the long, dreary years in the City of London were fading fast, or more accurately faded fast as long as he stayed away from his former workplace. Each time he returned, that feeling of emptiness, of indescribable depression returned. Back at Moorcroft, working among its colourful pots and cheerful workforce, he was happy. Sometimes when he was working in Stoke on Trent and decided that the time had come for a break, he would walk around the decorating shop or talk to the turners or mould-makers, often to remind himself why he was there. There was a hum about the place, a feeling that everyone was enjoying their work and the creation of objects of great charm and beauty, all drenched with history. At Richards Butler, a break from work would have meant a visit to the office coffee machine – nothing more. After that, it was back to the piles of paper, the time sheets, the marketing and the management of a multi-million pound global business. Moorcroft was his new workplace, and although he hardly dared admit it, Hugh was fast regretting that he had ever signed up to a consultancy agreement with his old law firm. He had an affection for his former partners, and he genuinely believed Richards Butler to be one of the finest international law firms in the world. Even so, his residual feelings of depression were not just accentuated by London. They were precipitated by London.

*Training pieces. Height of ginger jar 15 cm (6").*

# THREE

# Design Studio Lift-off

As meetings go, the Moorcroft Board meeting of 30 April 1997 was a relatively painless affair. Rachel needed hands-on support in her work. No one had any doubts about that, doubly so because all those present acknowledged she had shown considerable flair in her encounters with the media in all its forms. Rachel was 'a natural' as they say, and it was inevitable that she would always be one of the focal points of Moorcroft's media relations. One day, Hugh dreamed, the designer would take the lead as presenter on a television programme with all the workforce moving in to play their own parts. She had the media skills necessary, and after the pots themselves, there was nothing more interesting for a Moorcroft collector than a Moorcroft designer.

There was, however, something more for the Board to consider. In the interest of openness, Hugh decided to put his own very personal cards on the table. Although at the time it was only a matter of theory, he was more than happy to give every last ounce of thirty years of commercial, legal and managerial skills to Moorcroft, provided in return he could continue to supervise the design process on his own for a while. That would be his deal. It was not that he considered himself to be a designer. To suggest that he was would be silly. To direct design with a number of designers whose work was spread across more than one company, was a management skill. Each designer's work had to be kept separate and appraised objectively from a collector's point of view. Simultaneously, Moorcroft's design needs would have to be anticipated and then fulfilled within an agreed timescale, something that would become even more important if the Moorcroft name ever sheltered other companies in the applied arts. Put simply, Hugh was looking to the creation of a Moorcroft Design Studio.

In this way, Hugh told his colleagues, he would become the link between design and the Board. Rachel herself would head the Design Studio. Formal design evaluation would always be given at a design meeting. Generally, but not necessarily exclusively, those attending a design meeting would be relevant Board members and other senior Moorcroft personnel including the senior designer herself. After formal approval, pieces would be used as the Moorcroft Board directed. Hugh was happy with that proviso. The Board agreed, and their decision was minuted. After that it became even more necessary to identify the companies which would one day join the Moorcroft corporate family and require design support from the Moorcroft Design Studio. Until they arrived, many things remained theoretical.

*Rachel Bishop*

The Chairman's next push concerned the creation of the Design Studio itself. Hugh asked for and obtained full Board authority to recruit new designers, full-time, part-time and freelance without restriction. Like some of the other decisions reached at that seemingly modest Board meeting, the creation of a Design Studio was one of the more momentous, even revolutionary, decisions in the company's long and colourful history. For one hundred years, Moorcroft had relied on a single full-time designer; and in less than two hours all that had changed. If it worked, collectors would be pleased. If it failed, Hugh would take the blame.

As a commercial man, Hugh knew that he had no other option. Never again could Moorcroft rely on a single designer, whether to save costs or face. Increasingly, design was the engine which powered Moorcroft forward. Collectors had expectations. They applied pressure subtly for design changes to come about far more frequently than in the more leisurely days of William Moorcroft or much of the post-war era. With the Design Studio concept backed by a Board approval, Hugh set about implementing the decision. And his first port of call was senior designer, Rachel Bishop.

How long the huge, unfired RM3/27 vase had sat on the fridge in Rachel's Stoke on Trent studio, Hugh was unsure. It had certainly been a long time, a conclusion partially proved by the sundry cooking splashes over its ample body. The vase carried a design which made Hugh smile each time he looked at it. As a child, he had been exceptionally short for his years. When his friends at school were five feet tall, Hugh was only four feet. Only when the child emerged spotty-faced into its teens did Hugh start to grow with a vengeance. As a small boy, walking to and from school down Ryden Lane near the village of Charlton, just four miles from Evesham, his strongly-held recollection was of a forest of cow parsley. Hugh was too small to see over the top, and the real fun was to look for a bar of chocolate or packet of sweets which his father often hid for his son to find among the grass and flowers which grew in profusion under the cow parsley at the roadside.

From the very beginning Hugh had exceptionally sharp eyes, and seldom did he fail to find the prize on his way home from school. Sweet rationing had just ended, and confectionery was still a luxury in the school playground. The story struck a chord with Rachel who had drawn her design soon after Hugh had recounted his childhood tale to her. As occasionally happens in the life of an art pottery, the Ryden Lane design collided with Walter Moorcroft's After the Storm vase, approved as Moorcroft's prestige piece for the centenary year. As a result the unfired clay prototype Ryden Lane vase, all 69cm of it, had languished uncoloured on the designer's fridge for more than two years.

It was June, and Rachel had regained her old sparkle. With designer dog Murphy permanently in tow, her visits to the Works had become increasingly frequent. On one such visit Hugh once more broached the subject of a design studio. The two of them were already aware that Nicki Lee had mastered the art of decorating in the Moorcroft style, and Justin Emery, in consultation with Keith Dawson, had moved her on to learn the equally difficult art of tube-lining. At this juncture, Nicki's progress became less dramatic. In the way Moorcroft pots are decorated, a real sense of colour is a huge asset to the decorator, and Nicki Lee was a genuine colourist. Several examples of her colour trials fetched high prices over the Centenary Open Weekend, and Moorcroft collectors always cast their votes with cheque books or credit cards. Tube-lining, however, was an altogether different story.

Design outlines are pressed on to the still wet but smooth surface of the pot using tracing paper and a special tracing ink. Only when this has been done is the piece ready for the tube-liner. To apply tube-lining to the ink outline of the design on the pot is not unlike the process of icing a cake. The tube-liner holds a rubber squeeze bag full of liquid clay or slip. Affixed to this bag is a glass pipette with a very fine nozzle. When the tube-liner squeezes the bag, the liquid clay travels down the pipette from the rubber bag and onto the damp clay surface of the pot. Nicki the colourist and would-be tube-liner found the art of slip-trailing, as it is sometimes called, more difficult than strict art school theory might suggest, and from the outset she struggled. Doubts were expressed that she would pass the double test of decorating and tube-lining to Moorcroft standards.

With the jury still out on Nicki Lee, Hugh tried a different approach by explaining his own vision of the Moorcroft Design Studio and the reasons for its creation. Rachel liked the idea of recycling good designs into other art forms. Her own Poppy and Oberon designs had already translated into quality ties and scarves for Liberty. Many of them had been used for centenary presents from the company to Moorcroft's retail partners up and down the British Isles. Liberty had sold the remainder with enthusiasm from their Regent Street store, and although the Moorcroft designer did not know it at the time, Liberty planned to make more Oberon scarves in three new colourways for their Christmas trade later in the year.

Suspicious of his motives, the designer quizzed Hugh intensely on what he meant by 'other art forms'. Caught unawares by the directness of the question, Hugh decided to tell Rachel of the idea that had recently formed in his mind. Moorcroft had just started a novel and extremely difficult research programme into a wholly undeveloped ceramic process – a process involving potting and decorating techniques which were totally different from any used by Moorcroft. If the research and development were successful, the new pottery would need substantial design input.

It was also possible that Moorcroft might acquire a company with a real hunger for design such as decorative enamels. For good measure, he pointed out that there was also a strong market in greetings cards, wrapping paper and textiles too – the list was endless. The designer was still dissatisfied and pressed on with her questions. Why, she asked, was it necessary to change Moorcroft's shape and size so radically by introducing other companies or techniques? There was a risk that the family atmosphere in Moorcroft would be lost. It was a fair question, and Hugh went through his well-rehearsed theory of the pole and the pyramid.

After that, he moved on to tell her about the challenge of the unknown, the surge of elation at doing something no one had ever done before. Then there was the theory of waste, the discarding of discontinued designs. All these things together were less important than the fundamental truth that if you expanded and expanded production of Moorcroft pottery just to meet demand, you would eventually produce so much that the very essence of the Moorcroft name would be devalued. The company would simply implode and destroy itself. Unwittingly, some retailers, perhaps simply wishing to please their customers or impress their bank managers, were already applying more than enough pressure on Moorcroft to bring this about. No one who truly loved Moorcroft would wish let this happen. Moorcroft should never be diluted to satisfy demand, however vociferous.

So what exactly, the designer pressed on, did Hugh have in mind when he talked about finding a new method of making pots. He paused before answering. It was, after all, a highly secret project, but Hugh wanted to share it with Rachel notwithstanding. Moorcroft, he told her, was undertaking extensive research to see if there was any chance that stoneware could be decorated in an oxidised firing, as opposed to a reduction firing, in a way that still left a detailed and recognisable, fully coloured design intact. That was one of the last remaining unconquered areas of ceramic art. He feared that if he said much more his words would turn into a lecture. Instead, Hugh started talking much as he would have started one of his famous stories.

On the west coast of the Scottish Highlands, built on a headland covered in lichen-covered rocks, wiry grass, outcrops of purple heather and yellow gorse, is a small pottery called Highland

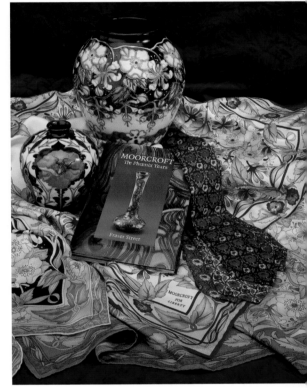

*Liberty ties and scarves*

Stoneware, so close to the sea that the roar of waves and the sound of grinding pebbles on the shore mingle with the bustle and clatter of potters at work. Twenty-five years earlier, Highland Stoneware had mastered the art of decorating stoneware in a reduction firing – a firing where the oxygen in the kiln is burned out at a critical temperature thereby reducing the atmosphere inside the kiln. The hallmark of Highland Stoneware's reduction fired pottery is the grey ground colour of the finished piece.

To achieve consistency, Highland Stoneware's pottery is twice-fired before the finished piece emerges from the kiln. However, the stoneware currently being researched at Moorcroft would have its own special clay body and would be fired three times in the kiln, not just twice. Even more importantly, the Moorcroft project would involve stoneware clay fired in an oxidised atmosphere where oxygen would be supplied throughout the firing cycle.

History had a role to play too. Another potter, William Howson-Taylor, had worked his art at the turn of the twentieth century after discovering how to apply high reduction fired coloured glazes to his pottery with dramatic and vibrantly colourful results. Hugh had no evidence that Highland Stoneware had learned this technique, but Howson-Taylor's work was brilliant by any standard. Potters had tried to decorate stoneware in various ways since 1300, and for six hundred years had largely failed. Some had partially succeeded in applying cobalt to a stoneware surface, but the impervious surface of a clay body mixed with crushed flint made it difficult, if not impossible, for the molten glazes to adhere. When stoneware was fired, the glazes melted in the white-hot heat of the kiln, literally running down the surface of the vase only to congeal at the base on cooling.

Towards the end of the nineteenth century, the four Martin brothers, operating out of Southall in Middlesex, and famous today for their mischievous 'Wally' birds, discovered that by applying sgraffito to outline the design, the glazes adhered more readily to the surface of the vase. The sgraffito design lines acted as 'ditches' and caught the liquid glaze as it fell. William Howson-Taylor took his secrets to the grave, while the Martin brothers left behind a rich ceramic legacy but very few documents of record. Interestingly, Hugh added as an afterthought, William Howson-Taylor called his pottery 'Ruskin' after obtaining the written consent of the famous poet and art critic, John Ruskin, to do so.

While Highland Stoneware was still alive, the Martin brothers, although dead, are still greatly admired for their pioneering, innovative and occasionally humorous work. There were lessons to be learned from all of them, but for Hugh and his small Moorcroft team of experts, the holy grail was to discover how to decorate high-fired stoneware in an oxidised firing which left a defined and fully-coloured design image intact.

Substantial progress had already been made in re-discovering William Howson-Taylor's secrets, and a few spectacular trials already existed. Even so, the foray into the past life and times of Ruskin Pottery was not seen as the main course but only the *hors d'œuvre*. The Ruskin glaze effects were fully re-discovered six weeks later, and a decision to continue research into the mystery of high fired, design decorated and coloured stoneware in an oxidised firing was almost certain to be automatic. Without forgetting Ruskin Pottery, the Martin Brothers or

Highland Stoneware, success would also involve developing techniques used by the late Bernard Leach in the studio idiom. But Moorcroft would move on and complete the process with the aid of computers and hi-tech kilns.

Hugh changed tack. If you love pottery, he suggested, the way to show it was to move technique, skills and raw science forward, bringing them all together to improve the potter's art; indulge in the elation at discovering something new; praise the achievements of others, and put a fresh dimension to the definition of creative design. Because of this, Hugh was unwilling to encroach on Highland Stoneware's preserve and follow their method of reduction-fired design. Instead he preferred to leave his own independent mark on ceramic history by pursuing with his team the technically more difficult route of oxidised firing as Bernard Leach had started to do, and he would do it on his own.

Rachel relaxed. Then why, she asked, did it always take Hugh such a long time to tell her that more design input would soon be required. The former lawyer was deflated and about to say something pompous when he realised that she was teasing.

So what did all this really mean? The designer was still reluctant to let go, and the man of words paused before answering. It meant, he said, that not only would Moorcroft have need of many more designers before long, but also that the company would be capable of doing many more things which required design contribution. The name 'Moorcroft' would go out to an even wider public, using different materials and different techniques. In so doing, the core integrity of Moorcroft's original pottery would be protected, as would the collections of those who had invested in it. There would be no need to respond to demand by producing more and more Moorcroft. That demand would be diffused over other areas of the applied arts, and the key to this was a Design Studio with Rachel herself at its head. What Hugh wanted to protect more than anything was that mysterious and special quality of Moorcroft which defies definition, yet which causes it to be collected, loved, valued and admired all over the world. The quality of the Moorcroft name, the brilliance of its images and the depth of the pottery's design skills would all be passed on to a wider public – glass collectors, decorated enamels enthusiasts as well as ceramicists whose vision and interest in their hobby travelled far beyond Moorcroft and the Moorcroft story.

Rachel said nothing for a moment. Then, almost casually, she asked Hugh for his reason for the change. Because he hoped that he had already answered the question satisfactorily, Hugh's response was expressed in simple terms, not easy for a former lawyer. There was not one reason, but two. The first was to secure the jobs of all those working at Moorcroft both now and for another hundred years; the second was to continue the company's reputation for innovation started by William Moorcroft a hundred years earlier when he married the seventeenth century art of slip-trailing to the technique of decorating raw clay with metallic oxide colours. Moorcroft was not a traditional company. It was an innovator, always seeking to improve and widen its skills. Moorcroft's role was to be a leader in the applied arts, not a follower. If ever it became a follower, Moorcroft would die!

# FOUR

# Scottish Mountain High

It was a beautiful loch, high up in the Sutherland Highlands. White cumulus clouds scudded across a clear blue sky, pushed on by a warm spring breeze which swished through the bracken and marsh grass at the water's edge. Hugh and Maureen had stopped fishing to listen to the cuckoos. Never had so much noise been made by so few birds in such a wild and remote place. Each call seemed to reverberate a dozen times off the steep hillsides that stood guard over the loch and the small green islands scattered across its surface. The next day the two of them would be fishing another loch close by with David Grant, proprietor of Highland Stoneware, based in Lochinver and Ullapool. The Edwards had known David and Norah Grant for some time and had even been guests at their home earlier in the year.

In their own home, the Edwards had a few pieces of modern Moorcroft, as most people would have expected. The only other significant pieces of pottery they owned, apart from Rozenburg, had 'Highland Stoneware' marks underneath. Highland Stoneware's reduction-fired pottery is one of Scotland's best-kept secrets, so remote is its location. Months earlier, Hugh had quietly decided to move Moorcroft into stoneware research. Reduction firing was to be employed as part of the exercise, but only as the means to rediscover the techniques of William Howson-Taylor and his high-fired, glaze-decorated Ruskin stoneware. Generously, David Grant had offered his expertise in return for a royalty payment, but that was not what Hugh wanted. If there was a new furrow to be ploughed, he preferred to plough it on his own.

While the highland loch cuckoos were music to his ears, several magnificent brown trout in the bottom of the Edwards' rowing boat were a fisherman's reward for the day's labours of both husband and wife. With trout in the boat and additional design support from a Design Studio in the offing back at the Works,

Robert Watson

Hugh found himself dreaming that fish might once again appear in a Moorcroft catalogue.

A month earlier, Rachel Bishop had taken a holiday on the Scottish Island of Islay. Soon after her return she had produced some tentative landscape drawings accompanied by an assortment of shells and seaweed. A strong design momentum was already gathering on her New Forest series, and the Islay drawings added weight to the senior designer's effort. Some of Rachel's trials had been delayed as a result of intense kiln activity following the huge success of the centenary designs. At least that was what Justin told her. Now there was even more pottery to fire in Moorcroft's busy kilns.

Keith Dawson arrived at Moorcroft in March 1997. Shortly afterwards, Robert Watson also mysteriously appeared, and within days had taken over Steven Swann's old sales manager's car. In truth, Hugh had sketched Robert's job specification to his wife Maureen and his fellow Board members. The free spirit as Hugh called Robert, would roam the length and breadth of the British Isles seeking out all manufacturers of stoneware wherever and whatever they were. The artist-potter that was Robert would then assess and analyse all that he found in terms of art, while the one-time manager that was also Robert would similarly assess the commercial viability of the new stoneware research and development. In less than three months after he joined Moorcroft, Rob, as he was soon called, had burned up more than forty thousand miles in a car that had already seen better days. The material he unearthed was without great significance in itself, but the possibilities for stoneware research assumed a new dimension.

For his part, Hugh continued to investigate the lives and times of William Howson-Taylor and the Martin brothers. One thing soon became clear. Howson-Taylor was certainly an eccentric person. Not only had he put a curse on anyone who dared call his pottery 'Ruskin', he also had the habit, so rumour had it, of burying pieces of pottery in boxes in the garden. To describe him as 'secretive' would be an understatement. Not surprisingly, the master potter destroyed all records of his life's work at Ruskin Pottery before he died.

The Martin Brothers had also been eccentric, but devoutly religious Plymouth Brethren who embraced the potter's art as poor men and died as poor men. Hugh felt that he would have liked the Martin Brothers and their strange ways as much as he would have found William Howson-Taylor difficult to understand. More importantly, he formed an unshakeable resolve to uncover Howson-Taylor's secrets. To do so he needed help, and the person he turned to was the hard-pressed Works' Manager, Justin Emery.

In 1996, Justin had re-invented for Moorcroft the old technique of 'engobe' decoration – it was frequently used by William Moorcroft at the turn of the 20th century to provide a base colour for the surface of the whole vase before detailed colour decoration was applied. Success was marked by the numerous blue 'engobe' pieces which surfaced at the Works throughout the centenary year as trials, as well as the centennial Yacht vase. Justin's reaction to the stoneware proposition was much more positive than it had been to an earlier suggestion to build a new factory to expand Moorcroft's lighting and export business. Hugh's first attempt to find a suitable site had ended in failure, with heavy legal and surveyor's fees to rub salt into the wound. No one could have known it, but the chosen site, at the perimeter of the old Sneyd Colliery, not only boasted a missing mineshaft, but was also unhealthily hot underground. Moorcroft withdrew from the deal.

For Justin, the prospect of stoneware glaze research forced out a smile. It was agreed that he, too, would make a visit to Scotland with a local freelance designer, Philip Gibson, to look at the work of Highland Stoneware. Philip had been introduced to Moorcroft by his brother-in-law, Trevor Critchlow, the company's mould-maker and part-time turner. From the time of their first meeting, Philip and Hugh got on well together.

Before the unlikely partnership of designer and Works Manager left for Scotland, Hugh issued a severe warning. If Highland Stoneware did something, it should never be copied or followed up by the Moorcroft stoneware team and used in their new stoneware pottery. About that the Moorcroft Chairman was adamant. It was an absolute rule. Soon after their return from Scotland, Justin set about designing and commissioning a new kiln to use in his research into oxidised-fired stoneware, one which was also sufficiently versatile for use in uncovering William Howson-Taylor's secrets of high reduction-fired stoneware. If the stoneware team of Justin Emery, Hugh Edwards and Robert Watson had known at the time just how many trials would be needed before success rattled the door, all three would have probably never even started.

*Bethanie Lewis*

Almost unnoticed, Moorcroft recruited a part-time employee to turn the stoneware trio into a team of four. Before the Edwards had returned from their holiday in the Scottish Highlands, they agreed to act as messengers and take a parcel for David Grant from his Lochinver factory to his Ullapool factory, saving him a round trip of some ninety miles. Sitting in part of the Ullapool decorating area was a young artist who tugged at Hugh's sleeve as he walked past. Blushing furiously, Bethanie Lewis told the startled Moorcroft Chairman that she had been offered a place at Staffordshire University in Stoke on Trent to read for a business studies degree.

To enable her to survive, she needed a part-time job, and to be a decorator at Moorcroft would be ideal. Hugh jumped at the proposition, but not before making it quite clear that at the end of the degree course the Moorcroft job would also end, freeing her to rejoin Highland Stoneware. A copy of Bethanie's offer letter was sent to David Grant, and in the absence of any adverse comment, it was agreed that the young Scottish decorator would start work at the end of September. It was unlikely that Bethanie's painting skills would have much relevance to the Moorcroft stoneware project, but even if they were only marginally relevant, it was better than no relevance at all.

With the stoneware research underway, Hugh was free once more to concentrate on Moorcroft and its design needs for 1998. The year after the centenary, Hugh had told a number of collectors during the course of Open Weekend, would have to be a very special year. The old adage that 'after the Lord Mayor's show comes the muck cart' had to be avoided at all costs. The centenary was fast turning into a huge success with the Moorcroft Collectors' Club membership climbing steadily, a success which many felt should culminate in a Collectors' Club centenary dinner in early October.

While Rachel was still working hard on both her Islay design and the New Forest series, her Ryden Lane RM3/27 appeared almost without warning from the glost kiln, full of colour and shining in all its glory. Everyone, not least Hugh himself, was taken completely aback. The huge piece was a superb mixture of rich colour, with cow parsley heads so real that Hugh felt they might start nodding. It was a magnificent piece of pottery, and everyone agreed that it should be Moorcroft's prestige vase at the International Spring Fair in February 1998. For the Moorcroft Board, the arrival of the Ryden Lane vase acted as a real tonic.

Less than a week later, when he saw the first Islay trial, Hugh almost found

FACING: *Ryden Lane, detail*

himself jumping around on cloud nine. It was fine work. Also hot from the kiln were early samples of a vase later affectionately known as 'Spike', and designed for use as the 1998 Collectors' Day piece.

Another design of considerable quality was also making progress. Rachel had drawn Crown Imperial on the 93/12 shape back in 1996. It was one of those mysterious pieces on which design work ceased before the centenary year arrived. The reason was unimportant. All centenary designs had been completed and there was little to be gained by creating a surplus design. Trials of both Spike and Crown Imperial appeared with increasing frequency over the summer until both reached an acceptable standard. It was the moment, Hugh decided, to concentrate once more on the idea of design support. This time theory had to be matched with action.

Before the summer Wakes holiday at the end of June, Hugh found his ear being bent from one side of his head to another by a senior member of the department of ceramics and surface pattern design at Staffordshire University. There was, the academic thundered at the Moorcroft Chairman, an exceptionally fine graduate named Nicola Slaney, one worthy of the Moorcroft design mantle so ably carried by Rachel Bishop, another of his graduates. Looking at her CV, Hugh decided that Nicola must be some kind of artistic Einstein. Eleven straight 'A's in GCSE had been followed by four straight 'A's at Advanced Level. Not surprisingly, Nicola had come top of her year at university! Before the summer was more than six weeks old, Nicola Slaney had joined Rachel Bishop as the second full-time member of the Moorcroft Design Studio.

Nicola Slaney

After Nicola Slaney's appointment several ancillary decisions followed quickly. Philip Gibson, still enthusing about Scottish Trout to Justin, suggested using them himself as a possible design theme for Moorcroft's 1998 year plate. Hugh agreed, and Phil started work for Moorcroft on a freelance basis. Two other freelance designers, Jeanne McDougall and Carole Lovatt, both made an appearance for interview. Carole had first helped Moorcroft years earlier when the Prince's Trust had suggested that Moorcroft resurrect Wemyss pottery. The project never moved forward, but Hugh's contact with Carole remained on file. For her own part, Jeanne's style was fresh and very different from anything seen in Moorcroft before. When the interviews had been concluded, both Carole and Jeanne found themselves on the receiving end

FACING: *Ryden Lane. Height 68 cm (27").*

of a request to bring forward new designs for consideration. In parallel, Carole started work on a Puffins design, while Jeanne took it upon herself to make a detailed study of coral reefs. Ironically, neither of them was aware of the Moorcroft plan to create a Design Studio!

# FIVE

# Flames and Hot Properties

Maggie Williams' invitation to Collectors' Open Weekend added a new dimension to the phrase 'quick response'. For the first time Hugh could recall, three collectors' acceptances were couriered back by motorbike! In less than four days the centennial Open Weekend Monday was full, and by the end of the following week all available places for both Saturday and Sunday had also been taken up. And there was more to come. The Collectors' Club superb Iris Jug, designed by Rachel for the centenary, skyrocketed in sales terms. In its first month, a greater number had been sold than Moorcroft's first two Collectors' Club special editions added together had sold in an entire year.

In the wake of that success, another production problem reared its head. Surprisingly, the Iris jug was producing a significant quantity of 'seconds', and Keith Dawson was anticipating a production run of more than 2,500 pieces before the edition closed with all orders honoured. While the ratio of seconds to firsts was nothing like the volume churning through for the troubled Yacht vase, the number was still unhealthily high. Maggie was advised to brace herself for complaints about slow delivery of the Iris Jug.

Eric Knowles, TV personality, antiques expert and raconteur, had accepted top billing as guest speaker at the Open Weekend centennial lecture. His knowledgeable and often extremely funny speech had collectors laughing as well as captivated. Younger son of William Moorcroft, Mr John, spoke of his father in a genuine tribute to a great man's work. Some of the anecdotal stories about his father passed on to Mr John by those who knew William Moorcroft during his lifetime triggered an idea in Hugh's mind. Because Mr John was only six when his father had died, much of the information about William Moorcroft inevitably is hearsay. What better than to ask a senior journalist to investigate William's life, his work and the man himself both dispassionately and factually? Several employees from William's early working years were still alive, with Patty Booth, a

former decorator, not only alive but well on her way to her hundredth birthday. Only a week later, Hugh was drinking tea with Neil Swindells, former features editor of the *Daily Mail* and a journalist with more than thirty years' experience behind him. Some new and original information about the William Moorcroft story would soon start percolating through into the Collectors' Club Newsletters.

A favourite occupation of Moorcroft collectors is to compete at Open Weekend auctions for the increasingly popular trials and staff designs. The centennial auction produced adrenaline in even larger quantities than the previous year. As a collector, Hugh particularly liked the blue-on-blue engobe collection showing a Hypericum jug, an Oberon teapot, a Foxglove vase and an exceptionally pretty two-handled Snowdrop loving cup. Drama was provided by a stunning and unusually coloured Yacht vase which roared through the magical thousand-pound barrier to enthusiastic applause from assembled collectors. With thoughts about the Design Studio still uppermost in his mind, Hugh found himself focusing intently on the staff offerings rather more than conventional trials and the rare dated pieces. Beverley Wilkes had consistently produced good designs for at least three consecutive years, as had Debbie Hancock, Angela Davenport and Emma Bossons – not to mention, of course, the great Wendy Mason.

That was it! The idea came to Hugh in a burst of inspiration. Key decorators or tube-liners at Moorcroft who were also proven designers would be invited to join the Design Studio. So in came Beverley Wilkes, Debbie Hancock, Angela Davenport and Emma Bossons. For her long years of contribution to Moorcroft colour, Hugh also asked Wendy Mason to join. From just one full-time designer at a time and only four full-time in a hundred years, Moorcroft now had seven designers including Nicola Slaney and Rachel herself. Unsurprisingly, all 'in-house' designers accepted the invitation. It only remained to decide how to deal with the freelance designers Philip Gibson, Carole Lovatt and Jeanne McDougall, all working independently in the city of Stoke on Trent. Carole already had a business of her own, which ruled her out. In Hugh's slim book of rules, some problems had a knack of solving themselves. Jeanne McDougall and Philip Gibson could wait for the time being. It was now time for the Design Studio to meet for the first time.

First to arrive was Moorcroft's official Designer Dog, Rachel's ravishing blond Murphy, soon asleep in a large 'carry-care' box full of comfortable bubble wrap and until recently used for storing trial pots. Rachel and her silk-haired

FACING: *Engobe collection*

ABOVE: *Philip Gibson*
BELOW: *Jeanne McDougall*

spaniel were inseparable, although Hugh had some mis-givings at its impromptu appearance in what was sup-posed to be an historic meeting. Stating the obvious, and with a wary eye on the sleeping Murphy, Hugh introduced two obvious truths and brought them to the forefront of the discussion. The first was that after the pots them-selves, collectors preferred to see designers at Open Week-end and on public occasions, and not directors or anyone else pretending to be a designer. Modesty is not a design-er's middle name. A consensus was quickly reached that 1998 would herald the start of Collectors' Days, with de-signers in attendance. The old style 'special occasion' events would become something of the past. Murphy wagged his tail, adjusted to a more comfortable position in his box, and went back to sleep. The designers accept-ed the company's decision that at Collectors' Days each should sign all pots purchased on the day by reason of their common membership of the Design Studio. In carry-ing out this task, designers would be signatories for Moorcroft, not for themselves. For a long time Hugh had thought it morally wrong for a non-designer to sign a pot, and that included himself. It was rather like stealing other people's credits.

No one was assigned a specific design task but all were asked to bear in mind the imminent Open Weekend and come up with new ideas. The meeting promptly sub-sided into silence at this point, and Murphy yawned. Indeed there was a sense of relief when a call came through and Rachel was summoned to move her car. Murphy sat up, jumped into her chair and, paws on the new boardroom table, eyeballed each designer in turn. Moorcroft is an art pottery, but even for Murphy it looked like the beginning of a new era. For the one-time commercial lawyer, accustomed to chairing orderly meetings of left-brained business people dressed mostly in grey, the first Design Studio meeting was a novel experience. But then the Design Studio was not a talk shop; it would evolve on its own.

If the truth were known, Hugh had probably fallen in love with the Tulip Tree with its large, flame-coloured flowers, dark green, waxy leaves and enormous seed pods. He first saw it years ago, its huge profile standing aloof from the misty rainforests in central Jamaica with its large, flame-coloured flowers, dark green, waxy leaves and enormous seed pods. In an effort to provoke a Tulip Tree design Hugh offered his own ideas and photographs to Philip Gibson just as he had done with Rachel many months earlier. Nothing had come from the Rachel initiative, but those who know Hugh well would not have been surprised at his subsequent approach to Philip in pursuit of the same objective. On holiday with his wife, Maureen, the year before, the two had seen tulip trees in flower for the first time. A common sight in the West Indies and parts of Africa, the powerful and dramatic trees add up to a riot of colour and organic form.

Less than a month after studying the Edwards' photographs, Philip Gibson produced his first design. Husband and wife were at loss for words. The design was both dramatic and colourful. At least that was the view of many of those who saw it, including Barbara King of Liberty, who described it as one of the finest designs to come out of Moorcroft for decades. After experimenting with the ground colour for a week or two, Philip settled for a soft moss green with a touch of brown to set off the vibrant red, orange and yellow shades of the tulip flowers themselves. After design approval the Board initially limited production to just four pieces, the tallest of which was drawn to Moorcroft's 92/11 shape. The design was christened 'Flame of the Forest', the alternative but apt name for the tulip tree.

It was still necessary to decide how to present the Design Studio's work in the Moorcroft catalogue. Hugh's suggestion was that a special Design Studio section should follow the limited edition pieces. Only a handful of pots illustrating each design would be used in the Design Studio pages, each carrying a special Moorcroft Design Studio backstamp. If collectors liked the pieces and looked for more, the design in question could be brought forward as a range the following year. Alternatively, a judgement could be made to increase the number of pieces shown slightly but still keep them in the Design Studio section of the catalogue for another year or more. Flame of the Forest became the first candidate for inclusion.

Once the gentler issues surrounding the arrival of Design Studio work in the Moorcroft catalogue had been re-

*Tulip tree, Jamaica*

solved, Hugh revisited the heavier question of Moorcroft's corporate shape. Nothing so far had happened to convert that shape from a pole into a pyramid, and it was now a priority that he talk to someone independent. His former partners in London were too far away, and in any event they had no knowledge of either Moorcroft's needs or the commercial climate in the North Midlands. Instead Hugh made an appointment to see Ted Turner, managing partner of KPMG in Stoke on Trent and probably the City's most senior chartered accountant.

Hugh spelt out Moorcroft's needs; Turner looked for the corporate 'match'. Many company names were examined but none suited except one, and that was Okra Glass Studios based in Brierley Hill near Stourbridge. While Hugh considered his options, and KPMG continued to make enquiries, suddenly, and totally independently, Okra Glass approached Hugh in the form of its managing director, Peter Hughes. A possible acquisition had literally presented itself. Life is like that sometimes. Okra Glass, with aspirations to be among the finest art glassmakers in the world, was on the market.

Competition for Okra Glass was strong. Its vibrant, brightly-coloured irridised glass was much admired by a strong retailer consortium as well as a sharp firm of venture capitalists. Peter Hughes had orchestrated a contest, and the key to winning the battle was master glassmaker and founder of Okra Glass, Richard Golding. KPMG were instructed to start that tedious process known as 'due diligence', with Ted Turner in charge. Okra was anything but strong financially, and occasionally Hugh was reminded of his own early days with a penniless Moorcroft during the late 1980s.

That said, Okra's irridised glass, made in the Tiffany idiom, was of the highest quality and eminently collectable, both for the United Kingdom and overseas markets. Mr John and Maureen backed the deal, which Hugh calculated Moorcroft could finance from its own cash-flow and reserves without recourse to a bank. Meetings were tense. Peter Hughes was sometimes in London negotiating with Moorcroft's opponents and sometimes in Stoke on Trent negotiating with Moorcroft. In the end, his task was to secure the highest price on the best possible terms. Contracts were agreed, figures and accounts were reconciled, but still Peter Hughes refused to say 'yes' to Moorcroft. Hugh despaired. He had seen all this before in his days as a commercial lawyer. Find the sensitive point and concentrate on that had always been his motto.

Translated into the applied arts, this meant convincing the artist, Richard Golding, rather than corporate man, Peter Hughes, that Moorcroft was the bet-

FACING: *Flame of the Forest. Tallest vase (right) 27 cm (11″).*

*Richard Golding. Master glassmaker*

ter bet. Both were invited to Moorcroft one last time to talk, and talk, and talk. Hugh decided how he would handle the meeting. Richard Golding was Okra Glass personified. Every last ounce of persuasion the former lawyer could call upon was directed at Richard. Eventually Peter Hughes stood up, indicating that the meeting was at an end. Hugh shook hands with Richard Golding and told him how well he understood his dilemma. Richard had to chose between Moorcroft's art, the commercial acumen of the venture capitalists and the strength of the retailer consortium, and how each might improve or detract from his work as a master glassmaker. Before they had reached Birmingham, it was Peter Hughes who called Hugh on his mobile phone to say that Okra Glass Studios would join the Moorcroft corporate family. 'Over to you, Mr Chairman,' he said, and rang off.

On 1 August 1997, the Okra Glass acquisition was completed. Initially there could be no design support from the Moorcroft Design Studio. Hot glass designers were a different breed altogether who worked to different rules, and everything made at Okra was 'hot'. Back at the Works, the initial impact of the acquisition was minimal – until the Moorcroft workforce, which was ninety per cent female, realised that the Okra Glass workforce was ninety per cent male. The subsequent arrival of a coach bringing some of the Okra glassmakers to Moorcroft was a highlight of an otherwise uneventful month. Hugh decided that for Okra Glass to move forward, it was imperative for collectors to identify a visual link between Moorcroft's pottery and Okra's glass. Until Okra undertook 'cold' glass design, support from the Moorcroft Design Studio was out of the question, but shape was not. After discussions with Richard Golding, Okra was invited to utilise such Moorcroft shapes as master glassmaker Richard Golding selected. Peter Hughes joined the Moorcroft Board as sales director immediately after the acquisition, but remained as managing director at Okra at the same time.

Jeanne McDougall was not a traditional Moorcroft designer. That much was clear from the outset. In July she produced for a doubtful Hugh to examine a strong and modern sea-horse design on a plate, as well as an equally strong and modern coral reef scene drawn on Moorcroft's attractive 102/5 shape. Whether Hugh was getting old or in mortal danger of becoming 'traditional' himself was difficult to say. At the first design meeting after Okra's arrival, he voted against Jeanne's seahorse and coral reef designs. All of his colleagues, including his wife, voted for them.

For everyone at Moorcroft, a Centennial Dinner was very much an unknown quantity. Kim Thompson, successful manager of the Moorcroft factory shop, Maureen herself and Maggie Williams worried about the likelihood of success or failure. Some collectors might find the word 'dance' as in 'dinner dance' intimidating; others might scorn the idea of a centenary celebration, particularly if it involved a high-cost ticket. At the end of the day, however, it was pots themselves that swung the balance towards a centennial dinner at the Stoke on Trent Moat House Hotel, with magician Paul Daniels providing the cabaret. Into the equation came a free centennial coaster with each ticket, specially designed by Rachel for the occasion in four different colourways.

In parallel, and taking a leaf from the Open Weekend book, auctioneer Peter Blood was invited to sell a few select and rare pieces under the hammer with all proceeds passing to a nominated charity, while back at the factory shop, two pieces of Moorcroft were made available exclusively for the Centennial Dinner weekend. Only three weeks earlier, and with a strong push from Maureen, the Board decided to use Jeanne's sea-horse plate and 13cm coral reef vase as the two special pieces. However, the defeated Chairman's jubilation at the decision to limit production of Jeanne's designs to the Centennial Dinner weekend was premature. As if to rub salt into the wound, the Board also decided that Martinique, as Jeanne's coral reef design was later called, would be produced in the Design Studio section of the 1998 catalogue on the 198/5 and 364/12 shapes plus the popular 8/6. After the Centennial Dinner weekend, however, the 13cm coral reef vase and the sea-horse plate would never be produced again.

In Moorcroft folklore, the Centennial Dinner

*Sea-horse and Coral Reef. Plate diameter 25 cm (10"): vase 12 cm (5").*

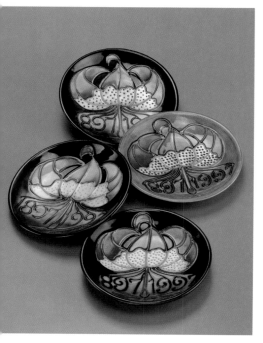

*Centennial coasters*

will go down as one of Moorcroft's great Collectors' Club functions. So many collectors decided to attend that the event had to be run twice on consecutive days. As some guests talked animatedly with other guests about their collections, others swapped centennial coasters, or talked to the large number of Moorcroft staff enjoying the occasion as much as anyone else. Their glasses clinked and laughter resounded from wall to wall. A charity raffle sold out; the auction was as lively as any ever hosted by Moorcroft in the past, while Paul Daniels, magician, raconteur and comic, managed to root a Christie's auctioneer to his chair and perform tricks with Moorcroft pots that made some collectors wince. It was an evening of good humour and fun, with a Moorcroft quiz tricky enough to tax the most dedicated collector to the limits. After all of this a few bleary-eyed collectors still summoned up enough energy to clear out Jeanne's sea-horse plates and the 13cm coral reef vases from the factory shop the following day before the last of them made their way home.

Unfortunately for Moorcroft, bad news followed the Centennial Dinner. After collecting her final design fee, Jeanne McDougall literally disappeared. Hugh investigated. To his disappointment, he found that she had joined another ceramics company in Stoke on Trent as designer, with an in-house public relations role to play as well. Hugh had no option but to write her out of the Moorcroft script. He had no wish to see a competitor take advantage of Jeanne's possible success as a Moorcroft designer. So overnight she became 'The Dark Lady', courtesy of William Shakespeare and his 'dark lady' sonnets. At the same time all three Martinique pieces in the catalogue became numbered editions and as such would automatically self-destruct on New Year's Eve at the end of 1998. From that moment, Jeanne McDougall ceased to exist as a Moorcroft designer.

Two months earlier, Justin Emery, Works Manager at Moorcroft since 1987, dropped his own personal bombshell. Since his school days he had nurtured an ambition to read for a mathematics degree. To qualify for admission he had taken appropriate 'A' level examinations and then applied to Keele University. A little late, Hugh had commented wryly, but he wished Justin well all the same.

FACING: *Martinique. Tallest vase 30 cm (12″).*

The former Works Manager would continue to work at Moorcroft until the beginning of the university term. With his pending departure, Hugh also saw a key element in his beloved stoneware project disappearing out the door. He doubted that Robert Watson would have sufficient skills or disciplined method on his own to see the project through. Once again Hugh was forced to call upon his powers of persuasion. In just over a week, Justin had signed a consultancy agreement with Moorcroft which tied him to the stoneware project until the end of the year.

Whether the emotional upheaval caused a lapse of technical concentration, Hugh would never know. Justin had 'glazed up' some experimental pieces, a few on old stoneware shapes, and others on a few familiar Moorcroft shapes. It should have been a reduction (flambé) firing, but something went horribly wrong during the night. At a point where the experimental, computer-controlled kiln should have cut out, it carried on firing. The precise cause of the kiln's malfunction will never be known. By morning, the gas jet had exploded causing the kiln's safety mechanisms to cut in. In among the debris in the interior of the kiln were five superb flambé stoneware vases, with entwined colours varying from grey to royal blue, fading to pink, then red and finally to a superb maroon.

Five of the Moorcroft pieces had shattered into tiny fragments but three miraculously remained intact. One particularly caught Hugh's eye. It was pure blood red flambé with some striking blue flashes on the neck of what had started out as a rather ordinary Yacht vase shape. Rob Watson had thrown all of the pieces into the waste bin as failures. Hugh, the incorrigible collector of all things ceramic and beautiful, pulled them out. One day, he decided, collectors like himself would be given the opportunity of judging their worth at an Open Weekend auction.

Later the same day, Hugh spoke privately with Walter Moorcroft. Eighty years old and enviably fit for his years, he had looked hard at the pieces salvaged from the damaged kiln before describing them all as 'superb'. It was praise indeed, but the sad thing was that there were no computer records to say how the result had been achieved. Hugh was reminded of the fable surrounding the invention of roast pork. On the first occasion, pigs in a house became roasted when the building burnt down accidentally. After several subsequently 'burns' it occurred to those involved that it was wasteful to burn down a house each time you wanted to eat roast pork. Thus it was with the experimental kiln, and an embarrassed Rob Watson was jokingly reminded of the fact.

FACING: *Flambé pieces. Jug 24 cm (9¹/₂").*

# SIX

# Designing Designers

'There it is,' Rachel announced to Hugh. 'What you see is what you get!' Crown Imperial had reached the end of the trial line. It was a lovely pot drawn to what was known at Moorcroft as 'the Edwardian shape'. They were referring, of course to the Edwardian years at the turn of the century rather than the contours of the Moorcroft Chairman. The designer's final colourway used a striking red set against a dark mustard or parchment colour. Mustard and parchment were considered to be the likely fashion colours in the run up to the millennium, a combination also used to great effect by Rachel on her prototype for a 1998 year plate. Even her Spike vase, already identified for use during 1998 Collectors' Days in selected retailers' premises, showed the influence of mustard and parchment.

Hugh pushed on with the plans to abandon the old-style 'special occasion' events. The Board backed the thinking and agreed that they should come to an end at the close of the centenary year. Collectors' Days, with designers in attendance, would take their place. The reasoning throughout had been simple. In the past, Mr John had acted as Moorcroft's representative at Special Occasions up and down the country. But the problem was that he was not a designer, nor had he ever been a designer. Now that a Design Studio had been formed, designers would be able take it in turns to attend Collectors' Days as Moorcroft's standard bearers and sign their own work on Moorcroft's behalf. As the creators of the designs themselves they were genuinely qualified to do so. From 1998 onwards, with a number of designers always available to replace an absent designer, there was less chance of disappointment. A substitution could always be made. For all those concerned, it seemed logical that Collectors' Days would be the most sensible way for a Moorcroft designer to meet collectors around the British Isles and, perhaps later, overseas. It was certainly what the collectors themselves wanted. As a result, Spike was refined artistically and technically to fulfil the role

FACING: *Crown Imperial. Height 30 cm (12").*

ABOVE: *Spike. Height 15 cm (6").* BELOW: *Summer's End. Diameter 20 cm (8").*

of the first Collectors' Day vase in 1998, and overnight 'special occasions' passed into history.

It was a complete luxury, the first-ever full design meeting decided, to have three year plate designs to chose from: the first from Rachel Bishop and the other two from Philip Gibson. One day, Hugh had teased his fellow directors, there might be even more than three to chose from, but catching his wife's eye, he subsided into silence. First a Dolphin design by Philip was shown round the table. Everyone liked it, but it was Hugh who cut the discussion short. Trout featured as a Highland Stoneware design: Dolphins did not. That meant that Moorcroft was free to bring forward trout art work whereas Cobridge Stoneware was free to consider a design theme based on dolphins. From that moment, the trial dolphin plates were designated as possible auction pieces to be sold during the course of the following Open Weekend. That decision made, the Trout design itself ready for approval as a Moorcroft year plate for 1998. Philip Gibson presented no fewer than five 22 cm plate trials, all based on his single Trout design. The trip to Scotland had clearly enthused him on the subject of fish as much as it had the Edwards. In what seemed like no time at all, the meeting decided that the best trout plate was the one with a mustard ground, shading out to blue at the rim.

Maureen, reflecting earlier comments of sales manager Steven Swann, was firmly of the view that Phil's Trout design was too good to use as a year plate alone. The others present all agreed. So what, Hugh asked, happens now? After a few comments like 'silly question', Maureen suggested that Rachel's pretty design Summer's End should be used as the 1998 year plate. Only a few minor modifications were necessary, and the piece would be an early candidate for production. Trout as a design theme would be reserved as a range for 1999, based on the mustard ground trial. Philip was delighted at the decision, and throughout the remainder of the summer and well into autumn trials of an increasingly impressive Trout range appeared all over the Works. By 1999, fish would once again be rep-

FACING: *Top left. Rare trial Dolphin year plate. Diameter 20 cm (8"). Top right. 1998 Trial Trout year plate. Diameter 20 cm (8"). Bottom left. Watercolour for Trout design. Bottom right. Trout vase. Height 40 cm (16").*

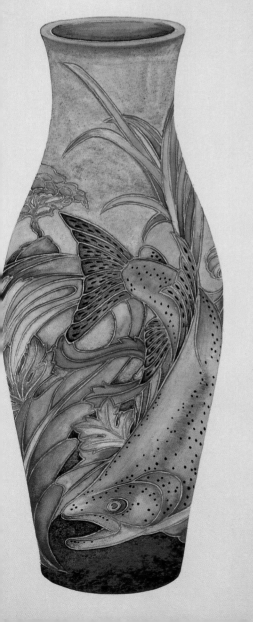

*Two handled Trout vase.*
*Height 25 cm (10″).*

resented in a Moorcroft catalogue in a full and very striking collection.

Only days after the design meeting, Hugh found himself eating curry in Brierley Hill, Birmingham, with Richard Golding, founder of Okra Glass. It was proving a hard task to introduce the large number of Moorcroft shapes which Richard had identified for his 'new look' Okra Glass in 1998. The whole process of creating a new shape in a glassworks seemed to be unbelievably complex. It was hard enough for Moorcroft mould-maker, Trevor Critchlow, to bring forward something new, but the dramas involved in glassmaking were on an altogether higher plane. No wonder, Hugh had been forced to comment, pieces of irridised Tiffany glass fetch such high prices in the great salesrooms of the world! Changing tack, Richard promised 'a big surprise' at Okra's own and very first design meeting, scheduled for the following week. No matter how hard he tried, however many traps he set over the King Prawn Korai, Richard Golding's lips remained firmly sealed. The glassmaker's surprise was to remain a surprise.

When the surprise was revealed in all its glory a few days later, the shock to Hugh's system was enormous – partly because of his long-held belief that you should never have expectations about anything, and partly because no one present had realised just how great a master glassmaker Richard Golding really was. Eventide was all Hugh could mutter under his breath. The vase was stunning. William Moorcroft's famous design had been translated into glass. If this was how Okra Glass was to move forward, any anxieties that the Board had about the company disappeared. Richard Golding acknowledged the plaudits and confirmed that the vase was a practical proposition to make. An edition of one hundred and fifty pieces would take a long time to close, but Hugh believed

ABOVE AND FACING: *Trout range.*
*Tallest vase 25 cm (10″).*

*Okra Glass Eventide vase. Height 22 cm (9").*

that collectors would wait. Those who were really astute would recognise both the quality and the historical importance of the piece when they saw it.

From the number of trials popping up here, there and everywhere, the home-grown section of the Design Studio gave every appearance of being as busy as the freelance brigade. Nicola Slaney's first two designs had not worked. She had produced for consideration two green pots with the design outline drawn on both, together with the required watercolours setting out her idea of colour for each piece. Both designs passed through for trialing, but the fired pieces failed to stir Hugh's collector's instincts as much as he would have liked. Curiously, he found himself talking to Nicola in much the same way as an enthusiastic but critical collector might have done. The lines were too casual, too imprecise; the colours of the main design feature were insufficiently distinctive; and the design itself had too many 'holes'. In practice a 'hole' was an area of the pot which had not been 'dressed' with design when perhaps it should have been. As the late Susie Cooper once said to an aspiring young designer called Philip Gibson, 'the spaces which a design creates are as important as the design itself'.

As a breed, designers are tough in developing their own art. Nicola resumed her work by going right back to the beginning. The result, which only just made the final design meeting, was her famous and haunting Amazon Twilight. It was an incredible piece of work from the Design Studio's newest recruit. Amazon Twilight relies on light for effect, and achieves the desired result with a subtle mix of greens, yellows and brown. It was a textbook exercise in precision. From that moment, nobody at Moorcroft had any doubt about the direction of Nicola Slaney's career.

Back in the fledgling Design Studio Nicki Lee was struggling and looked as if she would continue to struggle with the intrinsic difficulties involved in the art of tube-lining. Keith Dawson took the opportunity to speak to Hugh in uncompromising terms. Her ability to paint pots in different and unusual colourways was not enough to justify continuing with the original experiment. The Design Studio had moved on. Seven designers had been appointed, and the most that Nicki Lee could hope for was to be a competent decorator and perhaps a passable tube-liner. Hugh was forced to concede that there was probably nothing for her in the newly constituted Design Studio. It was all strong stuff and he felt

*Amazon Twilight. Height 20 cm (8").*

guilty. Hugh and Keith were hooked on the horns of a potential dilemma, but as sometimes happens, Nicki Lee took matters into her own hands and handed in her notice to work in a Night Club on the Canary Islands.

The youngest member of the Design Studio, Emma Bossons, grasped her opportunity to work as a Moorcroft designer with both hands. Although she had won a national watercolour competition, Emma, just twenty-one years old, had no degree to support her claims. She was an exceptionally talented decorator who had even been credited with high praise by Justin Emery. Emma had joined Moorcroft in 1996 at the age of 19, and from the moment she arrived, the young artist created a powerful reputation for hard work, inspired ideas and a friendly and popular personality.

From the outset, Hugh decided that he would see each designer separately to discuss their work. It would be invidious to have their efforts dissected by other design-

*Emma Bossons*

*Victoriana. Height 20 cm (8").*

ers, who probably had no stomach for that kind of thing anyway. Hugh liked Emma's Victoriana as soon as he saw it. Unusually it was a 'wrap' design, rare in Moorcroft, where the more organic 'growing' and 'hanging' designs have tended to feature strongly throughout its hundred-year history. The vase evoked ideas of a by-gone age with its delicately entwined chrysanthemums, Scotch roses and winter aconite, and Hugh's tummy gave that unmistakable flutter as soon as he set eyes on it. What particularly caught his eye was the subtle orange rim and base which faded into a dark, almost black woodsmoke towards the centre of the vase to great effect. Difficult to tube-line and paint certainly, but who better to supervise decoration than one of Moorcroft's finest decorators in the first place? The search for a 1998 Collectors' Club vase had come to an end. More importantly for Moorcroft, Emma Bossons' career as a designer had started to move forward.

While the 1998 catalogue still lacked a number of important ingredients, the perennial issue of discontinuation had to be resolved. Without doubt, the 1998 offerings to collectors would have to be at least as good as those offered in 1997. Some of the centenary pieces were numbered editions, orders for which were scheduled to cease on 31 December 1997. The existence of a closing date for orders had the effect of creating a built in self-destruct, and this applied even to the record-breaking Carousel itself. A real problem for Moorcroft at this time was to identify the true level of sales of general ranges. In theory, retailers world-wide had been rationed, with the Moorcroft sales team instructed to agree only a percentage increase over the previous year's trading turnover with the store in question. The opening of new retail accounts was out of the question.

One hopeful retailer arrived on the centennial stand at Birmingham's National Exhibition Centre in February saying he had finally decided to 'give Moorcroft a whirl' and placed a £10,000 order on the table. It was, sales manager Steven Swann said, quite impossible for the company to accept let alone confirm the order. Moorcroft already had well over two hundred retailers on its waiting list, and it was a list that grew by the week!

Rather as night follows day, if a significant member of new Moorcroft designs came in something had to go out. The William Morris collection had been designed to celebrate the centenary of the great man's death in 1896. That centenary was already history, and reluctantly Hugh realised that Moorcroft had to say goodbye to William Morris. Workaholic, designer, writer, artist and poet, Morris had cared for his staff and the conditions in which they worked. In that, Morris was a role model for Hugh to follow if he could. He had always subscribed to the Morris philosophy that true wealth was something a person made with their hands or which grew from the ground. Everything else which was said to 'make' money was an illusion. There was no such thing as making money. With those influences bearing down on him, Hugh deeply regretted the exit of the William Morris images.

It would be fitting, Hugh commented to his wife, for Moorcroft to replace Morris' Snakeshead, Leicester, Strawberry Thief and Golden Lily with something more tangible, more beneficial to those who were dedicating their lives to the company. What emerged from the discussion was a staff pension scheme, a scheme sufficiently generous to encourage all those who worked for Moorcroft to join the scheme and make comfortable provision for their old age. The pension plan had to be novel, something which took into account the fact that before many of those who worked for the company retired, Britain would have insufficient funds in the Treasury purse to provide pensions for an increasingly elderly population. To implement the idea, Moorcroft turned to the Ceramic and Allied Trades Union for help.

Just three months after gaining Board approval, the Moorcroft pension scheme became a reality. On 1 October 1997, the company committed itself to pay a sum equal to twelve per cent of staff earnings towards a pension scheme, provided the staff themselves paid a minimum contribution of three per cent. All were encouraged to extend their personal contribution to the maximum permitted by law for tax purposes, and without exception all did so. Thus Moorcroft continued to honour the memory of William Morris in a very tangible way. By introducing its pension scheme, it assumed responsibility for all those who gave their life's work to enrich Moorcroft's art both now and in the future. Even more significantly, the pension scheme was set up to make it totally independent of the company itself. In this way, the fund would be secure. No inept or dishonest Board of Directors in the future would be able to plunder the fund to cover up for their own incompetence or dishonesty at the expense of a dedicated work force who had saved for their own retirement and were entitled to expect receipt of a good pension at the end of their working lives.

# SEVEN

# Trials of a Chairman

The centennial summer slipped effortlessly into the centennial autumn, resurrecting in the process in-store promotions for Rachel Bishop and increasingly reluctant author, Hugh Edwards. Before autumn arrived, Rachel announced to a startled Chairman that she was pregnant, and that the baby was due the following May. Hugh was surprised and delighted all at the same time. Pleasure came mixed with an underlying and perhaps selfish anxiety at Rachel's outstanding design work for 1998. He need not have worried. Rachel announced that she planned to stay on until the end of April, health permitting. Ryden Lane was completed. So too was Crown Imperial. Her new and rather sobre wrap design called Royal Tribute was also ready. Royal Tribute was a substantial piece of pottery, its central feature being a vibrantly coloured collection of clematis flowers all set against a dark purple ground. Just in case Hugh had failed to notice, Rachel pointed out that a trial Royal Tribute was waiting for its first firing. As were samples from her new Passion Fruit range.

All 1998 designs had to be ready for photography by October if catalogues were to be posted to retailers before Christmas. It was clear that the senior designer had done almost all of the design work required of her. The problem was not one of design, but the trialing of designs in the Moorcroft kilns. For years Mr John had happily looked forward to the traditional dispatch of pre-Christmas catalogues. In contrast Maureen, the director in charge of Moorcroft's printing and publishing, saw no logical reason why tradition should rule in this or any other respect. Why retailers should want her to deliver Moorcroft catalogues in the middle of their hectic, pre-Christmas selling season rather than after the January sales, defied all logic. Even so, for the time being she could see no useful purpose in slaughtering yet another of Mr John's beloved traditions, however strong the underlying unease at perpetuating them.

*Passion Fruit. Height of jug 12 cm (5″).*

More kiln space had to be made available to accelerate completion of trial pieces in Rachel's Passion Fruit range. She had planned as many as fourteen pieces, but by the end of September only five were fully trialed and acceptable to the senior designer. At first, Hugh's inclination was to be mischievous and let the non-arrival of Passion Fruit provide the excuse for the non-arrival of Mr John's treasured and traditional pre-Christmas catalogue. Instead, he decided to change tack and force through all necessary trials himself. At the same time he would ask Rachel to complete the design work on an earlier idea which she had

FACING: *Royal Tribute. Height 25 cm (10″).*

ABOVE: Passion Fruit. Tallest vase 15 cm (6"). FACING: Passion Fruit group. Tallest vase 25 cm (10")

dubbed Swallows, inspiration for which had come from a number of chattering birds perched on telephone wires outside her bedroom window.

The new strategy worked. Within the following two weeks, not only had three more Passion Fruit trials successfully emerged from the kiln, but so had the first fired trial of Rachel's Swallows vase. The birds were perched on a tree with a rural landscape spread out beneath them. Only after looking at them hard for a minute does the viewer realise that he or she is the third swallow. It was an unusual design perspective.

If there was a second ceramic love in Hugh's life anywhere near capable of touching Moorcroft in its intensity, the name would be Rozenburg, a Dutch pottery which started life in Holland in 1883 before sliding bankrupt into historical oblivion in 1917. With its lively colour themes on terracotta bodies or unbelievably fine brush work on what was to become known as 'eggshell' pottery – so light, delicate and fragile that very

*Swallows vase*

few pieces survive to the present day – Rozenburg had all the hallmarks of timeless quality. The Rozenburg designers were innovative, the very opposite of traditional. Included in their subjects had been cobwebs, snakes, lizards, crabs – the list was endless.

Sam Schellink's Rozenburg birds appeared intricately drawn both on terracotta and eggshell bodies, but it was the design perspectives that set them apart from their contemporaries. Birds might be drawn from their undersides in a way that enabled the designer to show the viewer the delicacy of feathers beneath a wing or a tail. A particular favourite of Hugh and Maureen was a huge charger featuring a pair of partridges framing a flat landscape with their beaks and bodies. Only after studying the design does the viewer realise that he or she is the third partridge. Your perspective is the same as that of the birds themselves.

FACING: *Swallows. Height 30 cm (12").*

Somehow it seemed to Hugh that the spirit of Rozenburg had passed through more than a hundred years to re-constitute itself as a fresh perspective in Rachel's art. If design perspectives were timeless, here was the living proof. Rachel had not picked up Sam Schellink's theme, nor had she copied his work. That was absolutely clear. There was nothing in Sam Schellink's art which suggested that he was even remotely interested in swallows. Even so, his design perspective idea had been picked up quite independently and encapsulated in Moorcroft's art. In this way, inspiration and ideas can mysteriously weave their way from one generation to the next. The process is on-going. It never stands still or becomes traditional. If it does, it dies.

To watch Wendy Mason at work is an experience not to be missed on any tour of the Moorcroft Works. If Rozenburg designers were masters of perspective, then Wendy Mason is the mistress of colour. By consensus, those who work with her consider Wendy to be the finest Moorcroft colourist of all time. Not surprisingly, when Wendy is at work, random tube-lined designs can become a myriad of sparkling lights, with colour combinations so deep they look like a collection of precious stones. What she presented to Hugh on 22 June 1997 appeared at first to be a mass of swirling ribbons, whisked into life by a strong breeze. Of colour there was no trace. He studied her drawing carefully before asking what the paper represented. 'Just colour really,' was all Hugh could elicit. There was no colour on the drawing, but then the conversation was with Wendy Mason. The colour would follow.

*Wendy Mason, painter and designer*

Several trials of Maypole came and went before Wendy expressed herself satisfied with the result. In fact she was happy with not one but two colourways. Both were presented at a design meeting held at the end of July. Those present chose not to interfere, and Wendy's two colour themes were both approved on the impressive 101/14 vase as limited editions of 150 pieces each. Also approved at the same meeting were a ten-inch bowl and a 32/8 vase, each dressed with another Wendy Mason design. The bowl had been shown to Hugh much earlier, and it was he who had suggested to Wendy that in design terms, the 32/8 vase was simply her 25cm bowl tucked inside out! Moorcroft's famous colourist smiled and said nothing. Two weeks later Wendy's Rockpool bowl decorated

FACING: *Maypole vases. Height 35 cm (14").*

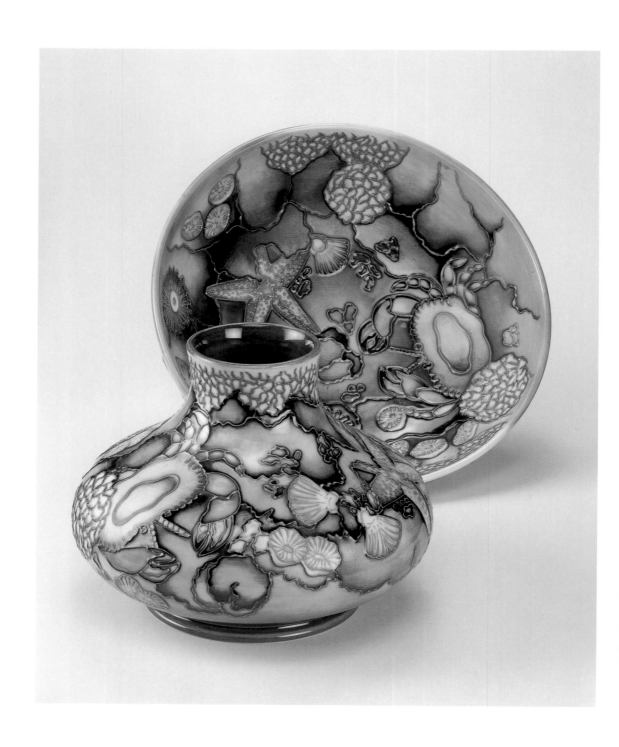

ABOVE: *Rockpool. Height of vase 20 cm (8″).* FACING: *Rockpool detail*

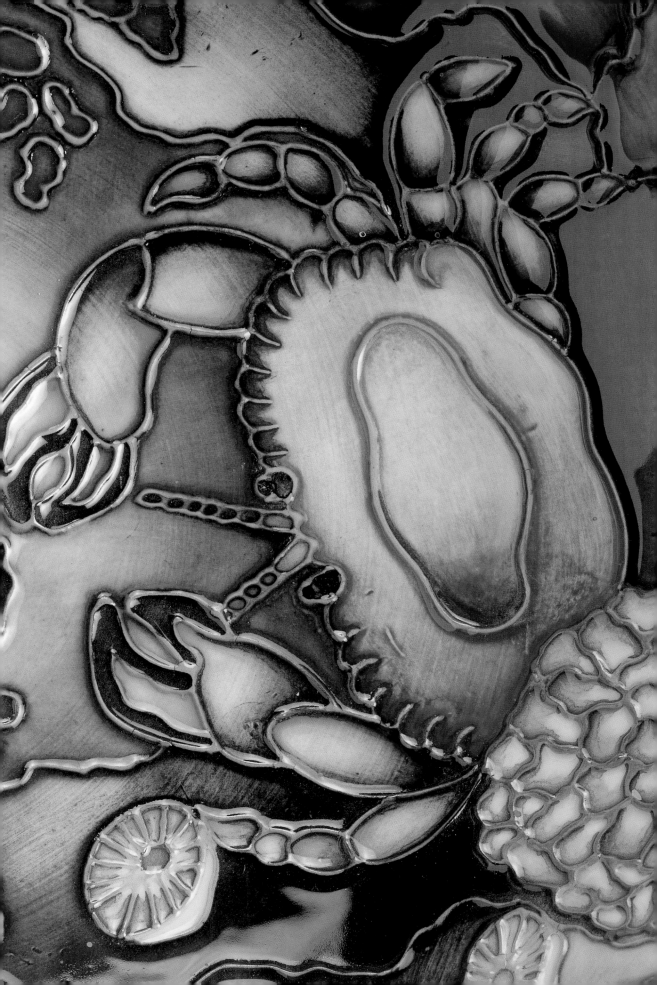

*Sweet Briar. Tallest vase 17 cm (7″).*

with crabs and starfish had been joined by a Rockpool 32/8 vase. Both were approved at the design meeting as numbered editions, and both promised to be bestsellers in the Design Studio section of the 1998 catalogue.

By mid-October the Passion Fruit range was complete. No one was in the mood to criticise or pass comment at the design meeting. For Mr John, fruit would be back in the Moorcroft catalogue, but the green base on each piece promised to be difficult to achieve in colour terms. Rachel herself was positive about its final appearance. Mr John looked uncomfortable at the mention of a potential colour difficulty, but offered his ultimate accolade by saying that it was 'traditional'!

Rachel was even more positive about Sweet Briar, her own special offering for the Design Studio section. The design was more than just pretty. Drawn to the 80/6, the 62/7 and the 99/8 shapes, Sweet Briar came in two colourways, the first on a washed lemon yellow ground and the second on a soft coral ground, not unlike Oberon, now bearing all the hallmarks of a design destined to be around for many years to some. Only later, after Mr John had supervised the layout of Moorcroft's price list, a task which he had undertaken for the preceding year or more, was it discovered that the prices for the Sweet Briar 62/7 and the 99/8 vases had been transposed by the Stoke on Trent printers in error. As a result, the larger vase became unbelievably cheap while the smaller vase ended up unacceptably expensive. By honouring orders made by retailers in good faith, it was an error which cost Moorcroft a substantial sum of money. It also killed sales of both pieces for the remainder of 1998. Only after the design had been re-drawn for 1999 onto new shapes could anything be salvaged from the wreckage.

FACING: *Sweet Briar*

*Wrecked bottle oven and factory shop*

# EIGHT

# Lightning Strikes Twice

In the unpredictable life of an art pottery, it is the unexpected which either brings the greatest pleasure or the greatest pain in its wake. From the time he first entered Moorcroft on 16 September 1986, Hugh's open affection for its handsome bottle oven ran a severe risk of passing into company folklore. Seldom did he pass by without giving it a friendly pat. To prepare for the centenary, a decision had been taken to clean up the factory shop and re-fit it to the highest standard. There were some who said that it was simply another exercise to favour Hugh's beloved bottle oven and put it into a special environment of quality. Perhaps with that in mind, local BBC reporter Barbara Adams had asked him what story would the bricks of the bottle oven tell if only they could talk. It was a good question.

For a moment in his mind's eye he saw badly paid and overworked men slaving under unhealthy and even hazardous conditions to shovel into the oven's gaping, red-hot mouth ton after ton of coal delivered in horse-drawn carts from the Sneyd Colliery, further down Sandbach Road. Those men would have laboured there for the duration of each three-day firing, the sulphur-ridden fumes searing their lungs with each breath as their shovels scraped and clattered on the hard brick floor. Their shirts and shorts (it was too hot for trousers) would have been black with soot and coal dust and wet with perspiration. The heat at the mouth of each furnace was intense. Mr William Moorcroft would have passed by occasionally in his tailor-made suit and bowler hat to make sure that every man was performing his allotted task.

There would have been a high price paid in human terms for each piece of Eventide or Moonlit Blue – a price not reflected in the few shillings paid to Moorcroft workers at the end of each week. Pay packets were usually handed over by the men to their wives to be spent in the corner shop on unsliced bread stacked on the floor under the counter, cheese wrapped in cloth and butter weighed from a huge slab. All this was a far cry from the prestigious Liberty Tea Rooms, where Moorcroft's powder blue tableware was used to serve tea and cakes. Those who gave their lives to Moorcroft creating powder blue tableware, Pomegranate, Pansy or Claremont saw little of the money they earned for the company. That much is well documented, while Mr William Moorcroft's collection of tailor-made suits is still the subject of comment made by survivors from that era, survivors whose words of historical record have now been taped in the interests of accuracy for posterity.

Before that, young William Moorcroft had been one of many thousands who had grown up in Burslem. Burslem people were real people, the backbone of Stoke on Trent's international reputation for artistry and quality. Via Sunday School and the patronage of some of the city's dilettante factory owners, William had ripped up his family roots only to attach himself to those who found the dirt, smoke and grit of the city centre too much for gentlemen to tolerate. Most factory owners made only occasional proprietorial visits from their handsome houses in outlying villages such as Trentham and Stone, but William Moorcroft appeared at the Works every day.

Yes, Hugh decided, those bricks would have told a story of toil and sweat, a camaraderie among talented people whose very existence depended on each other. These people would have enjoyed the long summer evenings together without television, talking in the streets, knitting on the doorstep, or watching their children play under a sky glowing red for miles around from the furnaces at Shelton steelworks. Their jobs were only as secure as the whims of their employers. Mr John often recalls how his father would sack the head fireman, Bill Bowler, on Friday only to re-instate him the following Monday. What a fun weekend that must have been for the man's family! One day, Hugh told the BBC's microphone, bottle ovens would feature in ceramic design as a testimony to this age of toil; so too would Stoke on Trent's canals, coal mines and steelworks. The list was endless. What he resisted saying was that Moorcroft staff were now among the best paid in the ceramic industry, and that one day, if he had his way, they would be the owners of Moorcroft and in control of their own lives as a result.

Before renovation, the Moorcroft factory shop was festooned with derelict electricity cables and rusty gas pipes, clinging to the walls and rafters like grotesque tapeworms, all smothered in flaking white paint. In the days when Gill Moorcroft had run the factory shop, this had been home, the place she would play host to dealers among a clutter of old tressel tables. In past times, the factory shop had provided a happy hunting ground for dealers with its dusty pots and assorted powder blue tableware. The Roper brothers, Andrew, Stephen and Michael, had begun to change the accepted order of things between 1984 and 1986. Pleasant green and cream packaging appeared, and the standard of lighting and heating in the factory shop all improved.

At the time of the current refurbishment, Gill had complained most loudly at the disappearance of the white walls in the factory shop. The wires and pipes were dispensable, but with a strong belief in her own will, she continued to insist that after sandblasting the walls back to basic brick, all should be painted over again although she conceded not necessarily in white. Sensing that he was more open-minded over the issue, Hugh successfully persuaded Mr John to wait until the shop-fitters had completed their work before making a final decision. Hugh had changed his position, the Moorcrofts complained. This was probably true, but only after he had seen the magnificence of the original brick walls. His strongly–held view was that it would now be a travesty to cover them up again.

The dispute seemed insoluble, and Hugh decided to consult the Moorcroft workforce. Without exception, they opted to retain the exposed brick work, backed with fittings of oak and iron. For a moment Hugh allowed himself to cast his mind back to the men who had stoked the hungry furnaces of the bottle oven. Through the votes of their successors, the factory shop walls remained as they were, with the bricks of the bottle oven now complimented by exposure of the same bricks used to construct the factory walls. In his mind's eye, Hugh saw the firemen and the placers smile. The bricks had told their own story.

Collectors' Weekends apart, Maureen Edwards had continuously resisted all pressure to open the factory shop on Sundays. Collectors were an organised and intelligent section of society, and what could be done on Sunday could equally well be done on Saturday or any other day for that matter. As a result, the factory shop remained shut on Sundays. This was perhaps just as well, because on Sunday, 31 August 1997, the mighty Moorcroft bottle oven was struck twice by lightning. The first bolt took out the crown of the kiln and cracked the stack, while the second blew an enormous hole in its belly. The damage from the thunderbolts and torrential rain was awesome. Bricks had been blasted sixty yards away, and the newly-fitted factory shop totally destroyed.

Ironically, it was the same day that Princess Diana was killed in a Paris underpass, which tempted the conclusion that God must have been exceedingly angry. Even so, in the factory shop itself only two vases were broken. A Lamia plate had flown several feet from its stand to land sooty but unbroken on a surprisingly forgiving brick floor. Fallen brickwork was everywhere. The factory shop roof sported a hole for each piece of brick that had blasted through it. The stench of wet soot lingered everywhere. More ominously, the tin hat brigade sifting through the debris noticed that almost all the bricks had fallen in the open spaces between the display stands and tables, exactly where Moorcroft collectors would have stood had it been any other day of the week.

*Kim Thompson*

It took three months to re-instate the shop to its former glory, except that this time the shop's new roof had a layer of steel mesh under the tiles in addition to a dark underlay and insulating material. For good measure, factory shop manager Kim Thompson lobbied successfully for air conditioning units which nestled unobtrusively against the rafters, veiled in the dark void above the shop's myriad of sparkling halogen lights. Hugh was less sure about the comments of the bottle oven firemen and placers on Moorcroft's air conditioning seventy-five years later. It was left to Keith Dawson to suggest that the men would have approved!

The lightning strike on Moorcroft's bottle oven was something which Hugh could have well done without. For a start, it completely threw out of focus his financial planning for the first quarter of Moorcroft's new financial year, which had started at the beginning of August, 1997. Additionally, both Maureen and he were still racing from one corner of the country to another to assist Kathy Niblett, Deputy Keeper of Ceramics at Stoke on Trent's City Museum and Art Gallery in putting the finishing touches to her Moorcroft Centenary Exhibition, scheduled for opening by Arts Minister Mark

*The factory shop fully restored*

Fisher at the beginning of October. Her title for the exhibition 'Moorcroft – A Hundred Years of a Living Art Pottery' appealed to the Moorcroft team. Visitors would know that Moorcroft was very much alive.

Cabinet space at the museum had been divided equally between all four Moorcroft designers, starting with William Moorcroft, then his elder son Walter, followed by Sally Tuffin and finally Rachel Bishop. Significantly, space was even provided to show Philip Richardson's invaluable freelance contribution to Moorcroft in 1986. By the time the show opened, Kathy Niblett's magnificently constructed displays were a credit to the city. Not surprisingly, by the time it was scheduled to close in January 1998, 52,000 people had seen the Moorcroft exhibition. In an unprecedented gesture, the exhibition was extended for a further three months. When it finally closed, no fewer than 106,000 people had made a visit. For Stoke on Trent's Potteries Museum, it was an all-time record.

Before the end of the summer, Rachel finalised design work on her New Forest series. Furzy Hill was causing considerable comment, all favourable, and Hugh already knew that Channel Four's Collectors Lot team had planned a four-day series featuring the design. When the television cameras arrived to film, it was Rachel who acted as presenter. The media skills and sense of occasion she had learned in Australia were only too apparent, but it was the men and women who worked at Moorcroft who also made their own special contribution by talking to camera about their work at Moorcroft, and through the camera to six million viewers. These remarkable people, lead by Rachel, were now front of stage, and Hugh was proud that he knew every one of them. Another of his dreams for Moorcroft had come true. Those who really did the work at Moorcroft were now taking their proper place for the nation to see.

Out of the four designs in the New Forest series, most who offered opinions preferred Vereley with its haunting bluebells drenched in moonlight. Holly Hatch was classic Bishop, and as a result it settled down in design terms after only a handful of trials. The same could not be said for Knightwood. After each trial, Rachel became less and less certain. It was time, Hugh suggested, to stop, pause and move back a few steps. Rachel searched the trial shelves and produced a Knightwood trial completed weeks earlier. Hugh the collector liked it

*Kathy Niblett*

very much and said so. After just three more trials incorporating only two modifications, Knightwood too was ready for Moorcroft's collecting public.

Rachel had limited the number of shapes used for each design in her New Forest Series to four. There was something for everyone. The series could move forward without tempting comparison with Walter Moorcroft's After the Storm vase. One piece of information, however, was now ready for the public domain. The first drawings of the New Forest series had appeared in Rachel's design studio more than a year before the arrival of 1997, and at least six months before Walter Moorcroft's first trials of After the Storm emerged from the glost kiln.

To be successful in an art pottery, financial control has to be both sensitive and accurate. Halfway through the first quarter of 1997-8, Hugh lost his financial sense of direction. It had been the costs arising out of the double lightening strike on

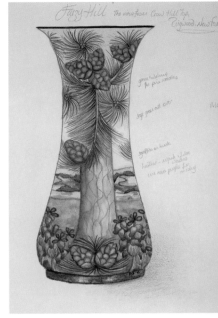

*Furzy Hill artwork*

the bottle oven which finally threw him, although extraordinary events such as the centennial dinner and the Stoke on Trent museum exhibition had not helped. It was not that Hugh had gone into overspend or had begun to behave irresponsibly on financial matters. The bottle oven was fully insured. It was just that for the first time, he could not see where Moorcroft stood in financial terms. KPMG, the company's auditors, soon sorted out the accounts and the quarter actually ended showing a healthy profit.

Key to the re-establishment of financial control was KPMG's local managing partner, Ted Turner. Ted was a popular and well-respected establishment figure in Stoke. Methodical, realistic, blunt and fair were the four words which best summed up the man. The time had come to seek out a finance director, and who better to assist in that search than Ted Turner himself, already at the top of his profession as a chartered accountant. As Moorcroft's auditor, he had always been there to support the company, beginning with Moorcroft's acquisition of Okra Glass Studios. The job specification for finance director was agreed but what followed was not what the Moorcroft Chairman had anticipated.

Just as Hugh had himself decided a year earlier in the law, Ted had found that there were no more hills for him to climb, no more goals to score in accountancy. As managing partner he had given his all and it was time for a change. There

FACING: *New Forest series. Furzy Hill (top left); Vereley (top right);*
*Holly Hatch (bottom left); Knightwood (bottom right). Tallest vase 35 cm (14").*

*Ted Turner*

was a chance that he might, just might, be available in nine month's time to take on the job himself. Hugh was over the moon. In Ted Turner there existed a man big enough and strong enough to see that his purpose in Moorcroft was to help put a whole new generation in place before taking the ultimate step of replacing himself, just as Hugh planned to do. And who better to help Moorcroft convert its corporate shape from a pole to a pyramid, and prepare the company for the advent of the millennium, than an ex-KPMG Managing Partner and a close relative of Stoke on Trent's most illustrious ceramic auctioneer, Louis Taylor.

With such momentous news, Hugh barely noticed that Beverley Wilkes had completed her design work on Andalucia. On offer were just two pieces for the Design Studio section of the catalogue, both on the 98 shape, the first 20cm and the second 28cm. Thorough to the end, Beverley had delivered more than the Moorcroft Board could have expected. There was less immediate pleasure at the arrival of Carole Lovatt's Puffins. It was not that the proportions were wrong or that the birds had been inaccurately drawn. The problem was that Carole had placed a purple pattern of geometric triangles at the foot of each design drawing, something which everyone felt required modification. With decorators and tube-liners working together, the purple pattern was removed and each design line taken neatly to the base of each piece. It was a minor correction, but one which so increased the impact of the design that it took on the hallmarks of a Moorcroft classic.

Hugh had a lot of time for Carole. She had helped Moorcroft in a major way on the Prince of Wales' Weymys project years earlier. At the time, he had no doubt that the company would have further need of Carole's unusual skills in the future. The truth was that Carole was a brilliant copyist and fitter. If Carole said that a design could never be copied and made to fit a particular shape, then that design could never be made to fit the shape. She could 'lift' a design from one piece and put it onto another in a way that no one else would ever think possible. Her eye was virtually infallible. Carole was a good friend with unique skills. Without

FACING: *Andalucia. Tall vase 25 cm (10").*

*Beverley Wilkes*

more drama, Puffins finally appeared on the 869/9¹/₂, 8/6 and 102/5 vases. Although Hugh was not to know it at the time, Puffins would join Martinique and Flame of the Forest as bestsellers for 1998. The poignancy of that particular fact was soon to become apparent. Philip Gibson and Carole Lovatt were freelance designers, while Jeanne McDougall worked for a competitor.

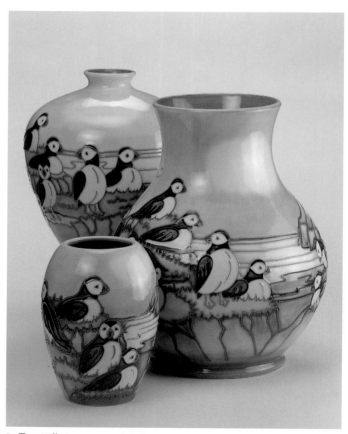

*Puffins. Tallest vase 24 cm (9¹/₂").*

# NINE

# Light Dawns

It was late February 1998. The roar of the surf as it crashed over Aitutaki's coral reef sounded like distant thunder. Between the reef and the glistening white sand that encircled the shore of the tiny atol lay a turquoise lagoon, so calm and cool that God Himself might have taken the water from heaven to create it. Protected from the midday sun, Hugh and Maureen lay in the shade of a massive coconut palm, the latter reading and the former writing, as they always did to relax on holiday. It was, Maureen remarked to her husband, not unlike one of the Gilbert Islands visited by the Edwards family some ten years earlier. Edwards paused, pen in hand. The island they had visted was called Abamama, and the Gilbert Islands carried the more ethnic name Kiribati these days, he answered testily.

Realising that a sensible conversation was out of the question, Maureen gazed across the white sand, past the point where the waters of the lagoon washed gently against it and beyond to the distant surf. The deeper the water, the more turquoise the sea became. In the far distance she could make out the flat shoreline of Tonga, still ruled by royal command and inhabited by a supremely happy people, many of whom were artist-craftsmen in one form or another. Maureen had purchased a small card made of wafer-thin wood. Using dyes from local plants, the artist had painted on the card a young man holding a shell-horn preparing to greet the sunrise. The tiny island of Aitutaki was part of the Kingdom of Tonga and would be one of the first places on earth after Kiribati to see in the millennium. If her husband was not in the mood to talk, Maureen was not in the mood to make him, and the Tongan card remained wrapped in its tissue paper to wait for a more auspicious occasion to be presented. What Maureen could not have known at the time was that when Kiriabti first saluted the millennium dawn two years later, a young Kiribati man appeared on television blowing a shell-horn for the world to see!

Two days later, Hugh the fisherman caught the biggest fish he had ever caught in his life. To land a 200 kilo marlin on his own in four hours at the age of fifty-six was no mean achievement. At that moment, exhausted, dripping with perspiration and deliriously happy, Hugh could have taken on the world. Instead, he was presented with the Tongan card by his wife. 'Birth of Light,' he puffed. 'Brilliant!' Maureen tactfully reminded her husband that she had offered other ideas during their holiday together. Enthused, Hugh pressed on. Kiribati and Aitutaki would see in the millennium more or less simultaneously. Both were on the early side of the dateline.

'Dateline!' That was it, he announced to his startled wife. The millennium would be celebrated by a Moorcroft Dateline series, with design themes taken from the collection of South Pacific islands scattered either side of the international dateline. The only problem was the identity of the designer for such an ambitious project. Jeanne McDougall, the Dark Lady designer of Martinique and an expert on coral reefs, worked for another company, while Emma Bossons and Nicola Slaney had never travelled anything like as far as the South Pacific in their lives. Both were engaged to be married, and both had strong ties to their home base in Stoke on Trent. Jeanne was the obvious candidate, with her skills in the use of turquoise and yellow already proven. As a result Edwards considered the unthinkable.

Nine years earlier, Moorcroft factory shop manager Kim Thompson had left the company to explore pastures new in the wide world beyond Moorcroft. Hugh, with all the guile of the experienced old lawyer, wooed her back again. If he had done it once, he could do it again. Every detail was considered. Salary, role in design, other duties, opportunity for travel. Then, quite by chance, or so Hugh tells the story, he and Jeanne bumped into each other at the International Spring Fair and talked. She liked the idea of travel and of helping Moorcroft and its image. The possibility of becoming the Collectors' Club Secretary for Cobridge Stoneware, if ever that particular dream became a reality, also interested her. Each problem raised was gently solved, each difficulty smoothly ironed out.

Hugh embodied it all in the offer letter of a lifetime,

Convolvulus vase. Height 17 cm (7").

and to his everlasting joy Jeanne succumbed, handed in her notice to her employers and offered to join Moorcroft in May 1998. It was all in vain. Hugh had secured Jeanne for Moorcroft, but May was too late for a trip to the South Pacific where the fruit and flower season ended in April. There was no alternative. Hugh approached Emma Bossons and Nicola Slaney and invited them to make the trip to the South Pacific as a designer twosome. Within days, Anderson's Pacific Way in Shepperton, Middlesex, England's South Pacific travel experts, had mapped out an itinerary, booked the air flights and made all necessary hotel reservations. Anderson's provide an accurate and cost-effective service. Moorcroft could not afford to leave anything to chance. The trip had to be a success, and the designers had to return safely.

*Debbie Hancock*

By the time April passed into May, Nicola and Emma were both back home. Debbie Hancock had already designed Convolvulus on Moorcroft's 101/7 shape for Collectors' Open Weekend. The design meeting liked the Convolvulus vase, and so did the collectors. All 180 pieces made were quickly snapped up, leaving a further 25 to be made to satisfy outstanding orders from those visitors to the Works who had failed to secure a piece during the event itself.

Much earlier, two of Moorcroft's leading retailers, James Macintyre & Co of Leeds and B & W Thornton in Stratford upon Avon, had each asked for a special limited edition. Their requests had coincided with the unexpected resignation of Collectors' Club Secretary, Maggie Williams, and as a result both were placed on a back burner while the implications of Maggie's departure were thought through. The idea of leaving her beloved Wales and the imminent arrival of her sixtieth birthday together convinced her that it would be wrong to make a long-term commitment to Moorcroft. To provide support, the Moorcroft Board had already appointed Elise Adams as assistant club secretary. It was now the moment for Elise to take up the challenge even though she was still studying for a Master's degree in the History of Ceramics at Staffordshire University. Her arrival in October 1997 as assistant club secretary had prevented over-worked Club Secretary Maggie from disappearing under a pile of administrative paperwork. Membership had risen sharply as the year progressed and was on course to double by

*Elise Adams*

the end of the Centenary year. Elise was computer literate, knowledgeable about Moorcroft and its hundred year history, but above all she understood collectors and how to work with them. From the day she arrived Elise worked hard, and it came as no surprise to the company when the Board appointed her as Maggie Williams' replacement.

By late September, the Sandbach Road Works were full. There was literally not a single spare place anywhere to sit a new recruit, whether that recruit was the Collectors' Club Secretary or anyone else. A new factory site had been secured in Nile Street, just round the corner from the Moorcroft Works in Sandbach Road. Formerly part of a large tract of land once in the ownership of the original James Macintyre & Co, from which Moorcroft had burst forth in 1913, the site had been used until recently as a Co-op Funeral Parlour. Above ground, it was an ugly building which cast a brooding shadow across the top end of Nile Street. Underground it was an infilled marl pit, from which pottery company James Macintyre had dug clay more than 125 years earlier.

Architecturally, there was nothing to commend the 1950s funeral parlour, and everyone at Moorcroft was happy to watch its demolition. Sinking the new factory's piles through the detritis of an infilled marl pit was altogether different. A modified North Sea oil rig pile driver of massive proportions was brought onto

*The new factory site, Nile Street, Stoke on Trent*

the cleared site and for three long days the city of Stoke on Trent reverberated to the thud of the great machine. Some piles had to be driven more than twenty metres into the ground before they hit anything solid. At the end of it all, architect John Sambrook told Hugh, the Nile Street factory had an underground structure which, in section, was not unlike a North Sea oil rig!

As Moorcroft watched each stage of the new factory's development, Mr John went a stage further and took photographs. One day the new factory would house Moorcroft's finance department, Hugh's own beloved Cobridge Stoneware project, and the first real Moorcroft Design Studio. Much more ambitious was Maureen's own project for the Nile Street site. Her plan was to create Stoke on Trent's first factory nursery – a place where parents working for Moorcroft and Cobridge Stoneware could bring their children to be cared for by fully qualified nursery nurses and teachers. It takes more than a year to train a Moorcroft decorator or tube-

*Underwood. Height 17 cm (7").*

liner, and Maureen's purpose as a one-time working mother of four herself, was to encourage mothers to return to work with their children on call close by during the working day. It was not altogether surprising that Stoke on Trent's near neighbour, Alton Towers, made contact with Maureen asking for details soon afterwards.

Among this peripheral activity came the serious business of making and selling pots. Once the problem of replacing the Collectors' Club Secretary had been solved, James Macintyre & Co had snapped up the opportunity of taking Debbie Hancock's subtle Underwood vase as an exclusive limited edition of 350 pieces. Drawn to the timeless 102/7 shape, Macintyre's had particularly liked the mixture of parchment, green, white and rich brown, which designer Debbie had used. Before the end of 1998, collectors were aware that for the second time the Leeds store had backed a winner with Underwood. So too had Thornton's in Stratford upon Avon. Drawn on the 95/10 shape, Angela Davenport's owl design was ambitious. The central design feature was a barn owl in flight at dusk. Again, the

*Angela Davenport*

colour mix was brown, white, and green fading to cream or parchment. Angela's barn owl was a powerful image, full of eerie shadows, water and distant trees. 'Elegy', Barry Thornton had called it.

For more than ten years, Talents of Windsor had been excellent Moorcroft retailers, often advising Hugh along with master salesman, Alan Wright, on do's and don'ts in his relationship with Moorcroft's retailers. Talents look after their collectors, educate and entertain without appearing to do so, and with each sale pass a small portion of their own soul on to the collector. Like Weavers in Saffron Walden and other good retailers, they supplement Moorcroft's own work in the world of collecting at the highest levels of the applied arts. In doing so shops like Talent's had already learned that most fundamental of all truths, namely that Moorcroft was not a 'product' functioning within 'price points'; something to be packaged by corporate man and sold with 'margins'.

Other great specialist retailers such as Macintyres in Leeds, B & W Thornton in Stratford on Avon, Just Right in Denbeigh, C.J. Beavis of Bedford, Weavers in Saffron Walden and many more, all understand the essence of Moorcroft and how to sell it. It therefore came as no surprise that Yvonne Hayward and Ian Herrod from Talents of Windsor should also ask for a limited edition vase exclusively for their shop. Sitting on a shelf in Hugh's office was a second Debbie Hancock vase, tentatively called Castle Garden. It was a lovely design with a subtle mix of orange, purple and shades of green fading to grey. For several weeks Hugh had debated how best to use it. There was no obvious role for it in the Moorcroft catalogue since the piece was just 8cm high. Yvonne and Ian enthused about the vase as soon as they set eyes on it, and in so doing accepted a challenge that no other Moorcroft retailer had even taken on. To sell an edition of 500 small vases was within Talent's capability, and Moorcroft was more than happy to release the design and let them try.

In the life of an art pottery, it is always the unexpected that can cause either the greatest stress or the greatest happiness. Since he was a small child, Hugh had always protected his emotions by never anticipating the unexpected. To be totally without expectation protects people from all kinds of extreme reaction through the elimination of imagined obstacles, fear or disappointment. Because

Hugh had not expected Liberty of London to put their considerable weight behind the launch of Nicola Slaney's career in their Regent Street store in London, the arrival of the invitation was all the more pleasurable.

During a visit to the Works, Liberty's Barbara King and Kerry Daley suggested that Nicola might attend in-store on 14 May, when her haunting Amazon Twilight vase could be introduced. Perhaps even more surprising was Liberty's request for an exclusive limited edition. And that, Barbara King announced to Hugh, would do nicely! What she had seen sitting on a shelf behind his desk was the first prototype of Nicola's Hawthorn vase. "Sheer opportunism!" Hugh thought to himself. "What a good idea!" was what he actually said to Barbara King.

There would be a formal launch of Hawthorn in September with Nicola making a second in-store appearance to mark the occasion. Even more encouraging for Moorcroft was Liberty's commitment to test-market the first pieces of Cobridge Stoneware. Hugh had no real idea when the Cobridge team would have samples ready, but it was agreed that if possible the Nicola Slaney promotion in May would be as good an opportunity as any.

Nicola herself had designed Periwinkle and Cowberry for Cobridge. Although simple designs, they reflected Cobridge Stoneware's progress at the time. There would be a Liberty press invitation for the May event with a unique opportunity for a double exposure of Cobridge, both in May and September. In a nutshell, Hugh had traded Hawthorn as an exclusive limited edition for a test-market facility for Cobridge Stoneware, behind which scientific and artistic momentum was gathering pace. The time to consider the imminent arrival of a ceramic never seen

ABOVE: *Elegy. Height 25 cm (10")*.
BELOW: *Castle Garden. Height 7 cm (3")*

*Hawthorn for Liberty.*
*Height 20 cm (8").*

before, one which potters had tried to create with mixed success for more than six hundred years, had almost arrived.

By this time the Cobridge Stoneware project was developing on two fronts. First, the team had successfully uncovered the secrets which Ruskin Pottery's William Howson-Taylor had taken to his grave in 1935. This was a goal in itself, but it was not the Cobridge team's ultimate goal by any stretch of the imagination. There was still the mystery of decorating and firing stoneware in an oxidised firing with a fully-coloured design image intact. Partially clear images were already available, but there was still a long way to go. Custodian of the greatest collection of stoneware in the world was the British Museum, their display cabinets full of examples of both moderate decorating success and moderate failure. Some had partially succeeded by applying cobalt to stoneware surfaces– itself a commodity more precious than gold in years gone by.

Sophisticated, computer-controlled kilns had not been available to stoneware potters in past centuries, any more than they had been to William Howson-Taylor. Only recently had art and science started to come together. For Cobridge Stoneware, everything depended on the final design of the gas-fired stoneware kiln in the Cobridge factory. It would be unlike anything seen before with its battery of computers, knobs, pipes and dials. Only control of the kiln stood between Nicola Slaney's Periwinkle and Cowberry designs and the appearance of the remainder of the decorated stoneware to be test-marketed at Liberty. To commit Moorcroft to an event unveiling Cobridge Stoneware at Liberty in May was a gamble. Hugh decided to take it.

# TEN

# Growing Pains

The 1998 International Spring Fair at Birmingham created an almost surreal environment for Moorcroft. There had been substantial over-selling of the Centenary Carousel and the hapless William Moorcroft Yacht vase. Works Manager Keith Dawson forecast completion of Moorcroft's backlog of orders by the end of July, but that forecast specifically excluded the Carousel charger and the Yacht vase. The Charger was both beautiful and popular. Once the apple of his eye, the Yacht vase, in Hugh's view, was in danger of becoming an albatross which might hang heavily round Moorcroft's neck for months if not years to come. For each good piece that emerged from the kiln, seven pieces emerged 'almost perfect' as Kim Thompson delicately put it.

It had been Kim's job as factory shop manager to dispose of the 'almost perfect' Yacht vases, and at each Moorcroft sale in both January and July more and more pieces had their prices reduced to a level which not only caused Moorcroft to bleed financially but which the Board feared might also devalue those pieces in the hands of collectors oblivious to the design fault which had caused the production problems in the first place. There had also been intermittent difficulties with Walter Moorcroft's After the Storm vase – a piece which was already selling in the secondary market at a premium.

To solve each problem as it arose, Keith Dawson followed the thinking of his predecessor Justin Emery and made special After the Storm trials on the 95/10 shape – identical to its larger brother in contour and design, differing only in size. It was difficult to calculate how many trial After the Storm vases had been made. Eventually, Keith gave up trying. His tentative conclusion was that more than 50 but fewer than 100 had been made before all problems were solved. Inevitably those trials themselves would also become seriously collectable, but if Walter Moorcroft ever designed again, sensible precautions would include a smaller version of the approved piece on which colour problems could be solved

*After the Storm trial. Height 25 cm (10").*

without recourse to the use of the word 'trial'.

What astounded everyone who attended the 1998 Spring Fair at Birmingham was the total sell-out of Rachel Bishop's massive 69cm Ryden Lane limited edition vase. It was a complicated design, heavy on tube-lining, heavy on decoration and consequently heavy on price. Even so, the vase remained Hugh's personal favourite. The piece was part of his own past life, the part that pre-dated his legal years. It was also the part to which he longed to return, recapture lost images and preserve them. Hugh the writer, lawyer and man of words had his roots in Ryden Lane.

It was, however, forests rather than flowers which preoccupied Hugh's thoughts at Birmingham. Demand for Philip Gibson's modest offering of Flame of the Forest was impressive. Collectors who understand Moorcroft's art openly endorse the opinion that Philip's design was the best to emerge from the company for upwards of seventy years, and as such a benchmark for future design standards. Pre-eminent among those who offered praise were Liberty, whose knowledge of and connection with Moorcroft stretches back to the end of the nineteenth century. A freelance designer with a Master's degree and totally independent, Philip had been a designer for Josiah Wedgwood and William Adams for nine years. During his time at William Adams he is proud to recall that he worked alongside the late Susie Cooper in what proved to be her final years at Wedgwood. After twelve years he had left to pursue his own career.

There was also a family tie between Moorcroft and Philip Gibson in Moorcroft's mould-maker Trevor Critchlow, whose sister Ruth had married Philip in 1981. Bringing Jeanne McDougall into the Moorcroft Design Studio, complete with her own Master's degree, had been seen as an achievement. To bring in Philip Gibson as well was too much to hope for. Phil, as everyone calls him, had done superb work for Royal Worcester, Wedgwood and Portmeirion, to name only a few. He had also introduced successful stoneware designs to keep company. Of these, the most significant Nicola Slaney's Periwinkle and Cowberry was Cobridge Stoneware's anchor design entitled Cobridge. Phil also designed the hugely popular Cauldon Lock limited edition, and the graceful Hosta design. Designs for a more than promising Moorcroft range featuring trout were already well advanced. Whichever way you looked at it, Phil would be a valuable Moorcroft asset; but like all good fishermen Hugh decided to bide his time before striking.

As the start of Rachel's maternity leave became imminent it occurred to her that Islay might benefit from one or two small design modifications. Unfortunately, it was at this precise moment that sales manager Steven Swann described Rachel's Islay design as 'Puffins without the Puffins', a thoughtless comment that had no basis in fact or design reality. The Islay concept had been conceived months before Puffins had even been suggested as a design. Design inspiration had arrived while Rachel was holidaying on Islay the previous summer. Whether as a direct result of the Puffins comment or not, and already eight months pregnant, Rachel consigned Islay to a top shelf in her studio where it remained until the end of her maternity leave.

*Flame of the Forest. Tall vase 12 cm (5").*

Even though Rachel had given her permission to be contacted during her maternity leave, everyone deemed it best to leave her in peace. The number of occasions on which she was asked whether or not she would like to attend design meetings were few. Even so, while Rachel was away the winds of change blew hard at Moorcroft. The biggest change of all was the arrival of Kingsley Enamels into the Moorcroft corporate family, with its twenty-five year old Managing Director, Elliot Hall. Moorcroft had purchased Kingsley in early August, almost exactly twelve months after its acquisition of Okra Glass. Hugh knew of the Islay episode, and towards the end of the summer responded with alacrity to the senior designer's suggestion that she might return part-time after her maternity leave to complete the minor alterations she considered necessary. Rachel was

*The Puffin range. Twin handled vase 33 cm (13").*

also eager to turn her hand to Cobridge Stoneware and Kingsley Enamels.

When Jeanne McDougall presented herself for duty at Moorcroft on 11 May 1998, there was literally nowhere to seat her in the Works, and the new Nile Street factory was running two weeks behind schedule. Some new space had, however, become available. The start of Rachel's maternity leave freed the building she had occupied since 1993 as her studio. In came newly-recruited decorators for training, including the first Cobridge Stoneware decorators.

Because Keith Dawson had started recruiting heavily both for Cobridge Stoneware and for Moorcroft, the Works soon had more trainees than ever before in its history. A radical rethink of Moorcroft's traditional training strategy became necessary. Hugh, who equated Anemone Blue with the obsolete 11-plus examination, had always been puzzled at the continued use of Anemone Blue as a training design. Mr John would point out that it was useful for learning how to 'float' colour onto the unfired surface of the piece. Hugh was not convinced. For him, an ability to decorate Lamia or Oberon was the equivalent of a good quality decorating degree. Traditional logic seldom satisfies.

Training pieces were already being sold through the factory shop, enabling a reliable and strict system of quality control to be maintained. Decorators and tube-liners with ability had every opportunity to proceed on a fast track to qualification. Alternatively, a more leisurely route was available should the artist need more time. Speed in learning Moorcroft's art is not always synonymous with long-term ability to produce quality work.

For a collector who takes the time and trouble to carry out a thorough examination of each 'T mark' vase, lamp and bowl, it is possible to see which trainee tube-liners and decorators have the hallmarks of a future Wendy Mason or Marie Penkethman. There was, however, a downside to the new training scheme. Teachers are invariably talented and tend to come from the most patient and often the most productive section of the Moorcroft decorating shop. Soon after the new training scheme started, Keith Dawson saw his production figures falling as the teachers' contribution to production decreased. Eventually responsible retailers and even collectors themselves would articulate discontent and frustration.

There was a double-edged irony in all of this. Before production could be increased it first had to slow down – something difficult for the layman to understand. Luckily Keith Dawson was alert to the fact, and Hugh, as the line of communication to the Design Studio, found himself on the receiving end of a request for designs of small production pieces for trainees to work on as they neared completion of their training programme. Within two weeks, Carole Lovatt was designing thirteen new Puffins shapes, including a number of smaller pieces, while Philip Gibson set to work to draw some additional but small examples of Flame of the Forest. These little design rarities were snapped up by keen-eyed collectors as soon as they appeared in the factory shop. The special mainstream pieces were soon joined by a highly collectable set of six egg cups, all designed by Angela Davenport and featuring farm animals and poultry. Examples were snapped up as soon as they appeared in the factory shop, often by dealers who then sold them on to unsuspecting collectors at extortionate profit. Of greater benefit to hard-pressed retailers, Moorcroft trainees became proficient in decorating mainstream Moorcroft pottery earlier than would otherwise have been the case, and the traditional notion that to float Anemone Blue was the height of artistic ambition for a Moorcroft decorator passed into the company's anecdotal folklore.

Six factory shop egg cups

# ELEVEN

# Moorcroft Waxes and Wanes

If Hugh was consistent in anything, it was in his insistence that his purpose at Moorcroft was to put a whole new generation in place and then to replace himself. Ted Turner's task was to delineate the job specification for an art pottery finance director, and then recruit his successor. Those who knew this were not surprised at the latitude given to Elliot Hall at Kingsley Enamels but with that latitude came high risk. In his career, Hugh had watched more than one young solicitor hang himself on the long, loose career line made available. When he arrived with Kingsley Enamels at the age of twenty-five, Elliot had the opportunity to learn from the years of experience vested in both Hugh Edwards and Ted Turner. He also became the youngest member of the Moorcroft Board, bringing with him the skills of a family business which dated back to 1904.

In Britain, there are four principal manufacturers of traditional enamel boxes, and all of them were proud of the fact that their businesses are traditional. Of these Kingsley Enamels was probably the smallest, although arguably the best in terms of quality. Hugh's pathological hatred of anything traditional made Moorcroft's acquisition of Kingsley Enamels all the more surprising to a casual observer – unless, that was, the casual observer was prepared to think the unthinkable and watch while a hole was blasted through decorative enamel traditions dating back to the reign of George II!

There was nothing to be gained, Hugh opined pompously to Elliot, in preserving snuff boxes for a nation that seldom used snuff. The youngest director countered by saying that he had already introduced napkin rings and egg cups into the Lilliputian world of enamels. That someone else had novel ideas similar to his own surprised Hugh, who had only recently approved Angela's prototype egg cups as part of Moorcroft's art. Very soon after meeting Elliot Hall, Hugh had recognised the arrival of a kindred spirit, but it was when Elliot produced a miniature Kingsley vase, albeit with a lid and not unlike Moorcroft's 65/6 shape,

FACING: *Squirrels. Height 27 cm (11").*

*Four enamels from old Moorcroft designs and Rachel Bishop's Snowdrop (below)*

that the Moorcroft chairman was convinced. The piece, more of a vase than a box, was less than two inches high! For Elliot too the word 'traditional' was capable of being wobbled, if not pushed over.

Within hours of the arrival of the lidded vase, Elliot Hall had collected fifteen plain Moorcroft shapes for copper spinners in Birmingham to create replica pieces in miniature. Moving in parallel, and only two days after completion of the Kingsley Enamels acquisition, a full meeting of the Moorcroft Design Studio was called. What Hugh asked of each designer was much than Moorcroft had ever asked of its designers before. As many as a hundred new designs for the tiny world of Kingsley Enamels were required before the end of November.

Virtually everything in the existing Kingsley catalogue would exit, and in would come four designs from William Moorcroft: Pansy, Spanish, Moonlit Blue and the perennial favourite, Pomegranate. Mr John would act as guardian of the quality of his father's work translated into another idiom, while Carole Lovatt, shape expert extraordinaire, would supervise all technical detail. Emma Bossons was asked to prepare a full range of pieces from a new design she had drawn for Moorcroft called Bittersweet, while Hugh made room for Rachel to start designing for Kingsley Enamels on her return, should she have time to do so. What came out of it all was an adaptation of one of Rachel's loveliest designs for Moorcroft to date, Love in a Mist.

Other Design Studio members were given the task of designing to shapes in Kingsley's enamel box collection, with as many as ten new designs coming from each designer. Some designed more, some less, but by the end of November so radical was Kingsley's new look that Hugh suggested the company change its name to Moorcroft Enamels. Elliot Hall agreed, and so did the Moorcroft Board.

At the end of this huge design exercise Elliot did to Hugh what Hugh had often done to others. For the first Moorcroft Collectors' Club Christmas weekend Nicola Slaney had created a superb ceramic design called Christmas Rose. Afterwards, in early December, Christmas Rose reappeared without warning as a

FACING: *Birth of Light Year Plate for 2000. Diameter 20 cm (8"). Inset: Peter Harrison, painter*

*Elliot Hall*

small range for Moorcroft Enamels. The explanation was simple. After the last collector had left for home at the close of the November event, Elliot had been presented with a Christmas Rose vase which the Moorcroft Board had secretly clubbed together to purchase from the factory shop as a thank-you from his colleagues for all the work he had done. The young Moorcroft director subsequently liaised directly but covertly with Nicola Slaney, and the rest became history.

In addition to Love in a Mist, Rachel had been on the receiving end of a less-than-subtle request to design a special piece of enamel work as the first Moorcroft Enamels Collectors' Club piece. Although the senior designer was not yet back at work full-time, she agreed. The result was Snowdrop, a design showing this most attractive early spring flower set against a snow-filled landscape. When a photo of the pieces appeared in the 1998 Collectors' Club Christmas Newsletter, orders for both the small Snowdrop vase and its companion box flowed in thick and fast. Rachel was already taking the lead in the Design Studio. Significantly collectors sat up and took notice, offering praise with their wallets. More than 500 boxes and vases were ordered in the first four weeks! For Hugh is was a moment of pure magic. Rachel was back in action. A year later, more than a thousand Snowdrop pieces had been sold.

As soon as Emma Bossons and Nicola Slaney returned from their voyage to the South Pacific, new Moorcroft designs started to flow in. Taking her first inspiration from the 'Birth of Light' card Maureen Edwards had carried back from her visit to Aitutaki earlier in the year, Nicola created a totally new design image to fit the ceramic idiom. The final colour work was completely changed and then enriched by Wendy Mason in a way that only the great Moorcroft colourist could do. The result, taken together with Nicola's fine line work, was what many now believe to be Moorcroft's best year plate. Halfway up a coconut palm, a boy can be seen blowing a shell horn. With considerable difficulty, Hugh had carried a large shell-horn all the way back from Tonga to assist in the design process. For Wendy, the shell provided a colour aid; for Nicola a line aid. The final trial showed an image as haunting and as wonderful as anyone at Moorcroft had ever seen, and the introduction of the piece at a September design meeting reduced all those present to total silence.

The same design meeting unveiled two surprises. The first was earmarked as a 1999 limited edition, which already operated under the name Squirrels. Angela Davenport had struggled with the piece through three or four design trials. Even though the colour had been almost right from the beginning, the squirrels had proved exceptionally difficult in design terms. Anji's aim was to capture movement rather than present her squirrels in a rigid pose. On one trial a squirrel appeared to have become bat-like with webbed legs; on another the animals developed a dumpy appearance. Angela's chosen vase, the 92/11, was one of Moorcroft's more popular shapes, and happily on the fifth trial everything fitted together. The squirrels were moving, the colour was correct, and the proportions accurate. It had been a struggle, but Squirrels was ready for Moorcroft's collecting public. Ultimately it was always collectors themselves who decided what was good, bad or indifferent. In the final analysis, Hugh reminded a startled Angela, collectors paid designer's salaries!

Beverley Wilkes was also having a tough time with a totally new shape, the prototype of which Hugh had secured on his last official visit to Morocco on behalf of his old law firm. The contours of the vase were in the classic Arab style, and it had caught Hugh's ever-roving collector's eye on a market stall in the desert town of Meknes. Just two weeks later master mould-maker Trevor Critchlow had profiled the piece, and within days Beverley Wilkes had secured her first clay sample straight off the block. Moulds could follow, but a block 'green' was all the designer required. The use of the word 'green' to describe a damp clay pot always puzzles new collectors, but it is a description passed down from generation to generation in the Potteries. Nobody ever challenges its suitability, since wet clay can have a vaguely 'green' appearance. Certainly that is the view of Trevor Critchlow whose own special skills were used extensively to create new shapes between 1997 and the year 2000. The process of carving, working and turning is relentless and contiuous yet vital to the well-being of Moor-

*New shapes, 1997 – 2000*

croft. Change of shape and change of design are each as important as the other – something that bankrupt potteries have ignored at their peril.

While Beverley worked on her Meknes vase, Hugh found himself in a meeting with Bob Justham and Peter Allsop of the Guild of Specialist China and Glass Retailers. At first he feared the two visitors would object to implications from Moorcroft's change in corporate shape. A stronger manufacturer was a tougher proposition for retailers to do business with. But Hugh need not have worried. The Guild were looking for a special design exclusive to Guild members for the millennium.

In some ways, Moorcroft was an enigma to the Guild. Its pots were correctly designated as decorated earthenware, not china, and yet Guild members were china retailers. At the same time, Moorcroft's pots had many of the qualities of fine china and a durability which more than matched the excellence of the Guild's mainstream china products. A decade or more earlier, Moorcroft Pottery was little more than tolerated in a Guild shop, but as the years ticked by its desirability and inherent 'good value' won the day. And Guild members made good retail partners.

Bob Justham and Peter Allsop as the Guild's ambassadors were a credit to their members, and Hugh enjoyed his conversations with them. Things were tight in design terms, the Moorcroft Chairman explained. The arrival of the millennium meant two years' design work in one for the second time in four years, and Design Studio members all had major projects of their own to complete. There was, however, the Meknes vase on which Beverley Wilkes was working, which was as yet unallocated. The piece was some way off finalisation, but it was offered notwithstanding.

Any residual reluctance Hugh had about offering the vase stemmed from the fact that the design was completely different from anything produced by Moorcroft in the past hundred years. In terms of colour, Beverley was working towards the Islamic palate of William De Morgan, a move which would compliment the very special shape of the vase as well as pay homage to its origin. If the vase were a success, it would be in everyone's interest to see the design on other shapes and sizes. The decision to go with the Guild blocked that option for 1999, but it was an option Hugh vowed not to forget, however intense the activity churning inside the Design Studio.

FACING: *Meknes vase. Height 22 cm. (9").*

# TWELVE

# Designers Blossom

Flair, talent and ambition rarely combine. However, Nicola Slaney, fresh from her triumphant partnership with Wendy Mason on the millennium plate, had seen a gap in the Moorcroft presentation for 1999 and produced a second 20cm year plate. The deep red lilies worked strongly against a washed green/grey and mustard ground. Hugh was delighted – until, that is, he realised both the millennium plate and the 1999 Tiger Lily year plate would be on the sales team's list for 1999. Maureen had long since convinced her husband that Moorcroft's millennium pieces would have to be available in 1999 for collectors to enjoy in their homes when the millennium dawned. Inevitably, many pieces would be made in the year 2000, but the arrival of Nicola's 1999 year plate forced everyone to concentrate their minds.

It was time for Hugh to talk to Emma Bossons. Emma knew before she left for the South Pacific that Hugh's favourite flower was the Frangipani, and it came as no surprise to him to find that Moorcroft's youngest designer was already working on a Frangipani range. But what else? Seldom in his life had Hugh been seriously shaken, but this time he was, and with a vengeance. Drawing inspiration from two native flowers of South Africa, work on both a King Protea and a Spiraxia design was at an advanced stage. The shape selected for the King Protea vase had been profiled from a striking piece in the Moorcroft Museum. But where the museum piece was small, Emma's new vase was large – much more suitable for dramatic design work.

A quiet word of caution was necessary. By choosing to create a design around the King Protea, Emma would be inviting direct comparison with William Moorcroft's King Protea design which first appeared in the mid-1930s. If this comparison was favourable, Emma's reputation as an international ceramic designer would be assured. If she failed, the collecting public would find it much harder to take her seriously again. Much as Hugh had hoped, the young designer re-

FACING: *King Protea. Height 38cm. (15″).*

*Hugh Edwards with designer,*
*Angela Davenport*

Photograph: Courtesy of Sentinel Newspapers

mained unmoved. Her aim was to help take Moorcroft's art move beyond that of her illustrious predecessor. Only in that way could she avoid standing in the shadow of a man who had died decades before she was born.

Surprisingly, Spiraxia appeared first. Although the original design had been drawn to the 98/11 vase, a 7/7 trial with orange and red flowers against a ground of subtle shades of blue was the first to emerge from the Moorcroft glost kiln. With seven well-integrated colour builds, the piece sent shivers down Hugh's spine. Less than a week later the first Spiraxia trial on the 98/11 vase rested on his desk with a beaming Emma sitting opposite. One or two alterations were made, but none matched that first full trial. Hugh had no reservations about the piece, and offered his full support at the next design meeting. The sheer strength of the design was phenomenal, and lucky owners would one day realise just how fine their Spiraxia vase was. It was a great piece of ceramic art with all the hallmarks of a good investment for those astute enough to buy it.

Even so, Spiraxia was hard to decorate. Emma had thought about that problem, and produced a 15cm Spiraxia plate from the bubblewrap in her sample box. The small plate was a good piece of Moorcroft in its own right, something which Walter Moorcroft confirmed the following day during one of his frequent visits to the Works. It would be a pity, Walter said slowly and with purpose, to waste the 15cm plate as a trial. His subtle suggestion was that when Spiraxia came forward for design approval, the 15cm plate should take its place alongside its powerful waisted companion. What followed was inevitable. The Moorcroft board decided that the vase would be produced in a limited edition of 300 pieces, while the plate would be introduced as a numbered edition. Production manager Keith Dawson was delighted. At a stroke, he had a small but extremely attractive piece on which skilled decorators could work before turning their skills to the 98/11 vase itself. In the excitement everyone forgot about the 7/7 vase except Hugh. At heart he would always be an incorrigible collector, and for him the 7/7 vase was too good to waste. Visitors to the pre-Millennium Open Weekend would have a very pleasant surprise in store!

In the decorating shop interest in Emma Bossons' King Protea design was

*Facing: Spiraxia. Height 27cm. (11").*

intense. After all, Emma had once been one of their number. Odd remarks had filtered back before Hugh first saw the piece for himself. Better than William's design from the 1930s, dramatic, powerful, the best Moorcroft vase to have in your home to represent the Phoenix Years. Emma and Keith came through the door of Hugh's office together. The young designer had brought forward not just one great design but two! Emma was radiant, while Keith, master of Moorcroft's production, was smiling more broadly than Hugh had seen him do for months. 'Pity it's got to be just a hundred pieces', was all Keith could bring himself to say. Hugh the collector found his tummy turning a succession of silent somersaults, but because he said nothing Emma started to look worried.

'Brilliant!' was his first word, followed by 'You're an angel!' Keith was right. It was a tragedy that production of Emma's magnificent King Protea vase had to be limited to no more than 100 pieces. Retailers had done all that they could to edit out orders for the Yacht vase but demand for outstanding pieces was still strong and in one way or another had to be satisfied. It was a fact of life. Hugh was furious, but however much he fumed, the reality was that in addition to the Yacht vase itself, a number of Walter Moorcroft After the Storms were still out-

Spiraxia. Vase 17 cm (7").
Plate 15 cm. (6") diameter.

standing, as was the remainder of the beautiful Ryden Lane edition and Rachel's Carousel Charger. There was no alternative. A hundred pieces it had to be. The King Protea vase passed all design approval processes without any serious challenge, although Mr John suggested that a small leaf on the waist of the vase should be lifted further up the body. Emma nodded at the comment, and the final trial included Mr John's raised leaf.

Hugh was still seething. To be obliged to limit the King Protea edition to no more than a hundred pieces was a tragedy. Outstanding orders for discontinued designs were always awkward to handle, and to prevent last minute speculation discontinuations are today generally announced without warning. The Yacht vase was different. Orders had been placed with an expectation of delivery. Ironically, it was Moorcroft's sales director who suggested a possible solution.

Until the last piece carrying a discontinued design had been delivered to the customer, no orders for new pieces would be accepted or confirmed from that customer.

That was in accordance with retail practice. Those who wished to trade in the past should be free to do so, and Moorcroft, with the help of its sales team, would do all it could to ensure those rights were preserved. Taken to a logical conclusion, those retailers who had sold a large number of Yacht vases and little else ran a serious risk of taking millennium pieces into stock later than others; but it had been their personal choice. Conversely, retailers who pruned the deadwood of discontinued designs out of their orders would be the first to take Moorcroft's Millennium designs into stock both in 1999 and 2000. That was fair, and Hugh was grateful to see that his nose had been pointed in the right direction.

As always, the anger and frustration inside him died down once Hugh could see his way forward. Keith would

*Spiraxia detail*

carve up Moorcroft's production capacity and release finished ware to the sales team to distribute to retailers in accordance with agreed policies. Those policies now embodied the principle that there would be nothing new for a retailer until all orders of discontinued designs had been supplied. The sales team would edit retailers' outstanding orders; and the full force of the Moorcroft/retailer partnership would then be free to move behind those who played the game according to rules based on fairness and collector interest. Sometimes in the life of an art pottery it needs help, and on this occasion it was significant that most retailer partners offered all the help they could.

Shortly before the 1998 Open Weekend, Angela Davenport produced a water colour depicting white trumpet-shaped flowers for outline approval. Just occasionally, Hugh was guilty of saying 'yes' or 'no' to propositions without actually listening hard enough to the detail. There were some who found this habit particularly irritating, and Maureen often forcefully reminded her husband of the fact. The white trumpet flowers had a soft, soothing appeal which was why Hugh waved Angela toward the door with an apparently absent-minded 'yes'. Had his wife been present to translate, she would have observed that Hugh liked the piece very much indeed, that there was little wrong with the design presentation, and

*Angel's Trumpets artwork*

that he had noted Angela's comment that she had designed the piece as the Collectors' Club vase for the millennium.

Unfortunately for Angela Davenport, Maureen was not present on that occasion, and to say that Hugh had left her confused was almost certainly an understatement. Not one to be negative, and with her colleagues' support on the tube-lining side, Angela painted up the trial herself. Like Emma Bossons, she not only decorates her own work but also invariably seeks advice from the tube-liners. The result was one of those great Moorcroft rarities – a trial piece which emerged from the glost kiln absolutely perfect first time around. Designed to the classic 393 shape, Angela's vase showed the same large white trumpet-shaped flowers seen on her watercolour set against soft green and graceful hanging leaves.

'Angels' Trumpets!' she announced before Hugh had a chance to comment. It was an appropriate name for the millennium Collectors' Club piece. Elise Adams loved it, and so did the subsequent design meeting. As a result, for more than a year the first Angels' Trumpets trial vase sat happily on one of the glass shelves in the boardroom waiting for its call of duty in the year 2000, admired by all lucky enough to set eyes on it.

It was, Maureen remarked to her husband as he struggled to lift heavy bales of sweet-smelling hay onto a trailer, rather odd that Moorcroft already had its Collectors' Club millennium vase when there was no sign of a 1999 piece. Hugh had learned over the years that whenever he was working for his wife's sheep, he could get away with much more than would otherwise be the case. No, he had not overlooked the 1999 Collectors' Club vase, always supposing that it was to be a vase in any event; and yes he had talked to Philip Gibson on the subject several times over the past six or eight weeks. Almost casually, Hugh told his wife that Philip had accepted an invitation to join the Moorcroft Design Studio as a full-time designer. Privately he had been delighted at Philip's decision, even more so when the designer identified a new shape for a Collectors' Club vase which appealed to him greatly. Only two days later Philip had prepared a design to fit it.

*Angels' Trumpets. Height 17 cm (7").*

The chosen shape was smaller than several of its predecessors, and 1999 was already designated as the year when small was beautiful. The new 72/6 vase suited Moorcroft's purpose well. Trevor Critchlow, the company's overworked mould-maker, was also Philip's brother in law. So if anyone could coax Trevor into producing the new shape quickly, it would be Philip.

What eventually emerged were no fewer than four trial pieces of a Wisteria design, all differing in one subtle way or another. Philip Gibson was a thorough designer. He never cut corners, always producing at least one watercolour and a 'drawn' green (unfired) vase to illustrate his design purpose. For Hugh, all four trials seemed acceptable. Any new piece of Moorcroft seen for the first time almost invariably evokes a positive reaction in a genuine collector. Only later, when the first wave of emotion has passed, can the appraiser sit back and judge a piece objectively on artistic merit. Both Hugh and Philip decided on the same design colourway, but remained silent while the design committee, as the final adjudicators, quite independently selected the same one.

There was a certain amount of poetry in their decision. Emma had taken on William Moorcroft by using the King Protea flower for design inspiration. After selecting Wisteria as a design theme, Philip Gibson had done the same thing with another flower. It would be for collectors all over the world to indicate their approval, or lack of it, by the number of orders placed. As a footnote, Hugh quietly took Keith Dawson to one side and discussed delivery of Collectors' Club

pieces in the run-up to the Millennium. As a breed, collectors are essentially patient people, prepared to wait for their prize once an order had been placed. Delivery in 1998 had been too slow. In 1999 it had to be substantially improved. What Hugh received was a commitment from Keith to allocate more decorators to the Collectors' Club vase in 1999 than ever before. That year, not only would small be beautiful, but collectors would take precedence over all else.

*Tiger Lily year plate*

# THIRTEEN

# The March of Time

Her lost opportunity to travel to the South Pacific was not something Jeanne Mc-Dougall either resented or complained about. Her former employers had simply not been prepared to release her in time to make the trip, and that was that as far as she was concerned. What did irk her was the total absence of even a chair to sit on whenever she visited the Works, so over-crowded had they become. In order to work she sat at the boardroom table, occasionally reserving a look for Hugh which suggested that not only was it too crowded, but that the time had come for him to suffer too. Hugh already shared the boardroom with Collectors' Club Secretary, Elise Adams.

The Nile Street development had slipped a further six weeks behind schedule, and practical completion by 28 June had already become practical completion by 16 August. The contractor's most recent achievement had been to put a completely wrong roof on the new factory, and they were not at all pleased when Hugh insisted they take it off and start again. The ex-commercial property lawyer was on home territory when it came to a roof screwed to purlins which were never designed to receive it. For mothers and fathers waiting to put their babies into the new crèche, for designers wanting to work in the new Design Studio, for Cobridge Stoneware decorators working in every kind of nook and cranny throughout Cobridge and Burslem, and for the Moorcroft trainers and their trainees camped out in an old carpet warehouse, it was fast becoming too much. To crown it all, Hugh had arranged for Richard Caborn, MP, Minister for the Regions, Regeneration and the Environment to open the new Nile Street factory on 16 September!

Jeanne soon made her point and was given permission to design at home. Her job as Cobridge Stoneware Collectors' Club Secretary was not scheduled to 'go live' until the Moorcroft Newsletter was despatched to collectors in late August. Until then, there was no alternative.

Cobridge Stoneware Works
in Nile Street

Justin Emery had agreed to oversee the fitting out of the Nile Street factory during Keele University's long summer vacation, but because of the contractor's delays, this had taken him away from his work on experimental stoneware. A smart executive somewhere, Hugh mused, would have noted the stupidity of taking the principal technician from the stoneware project to fit out a new factory. What the smart executive would have overlooked was that the new factory would house no fewer than four kilns. Three would be powered by electricity, but the fourth and most powerful would be a larger version of the stoneware trial kiln. Its sophisticated battery of computers had been designed as replicas of the ones which had enabled the Cobridge Stoneware team to crack the secret of decorating stoneware in an oxidised firing, as well as rediscovering William Howson-Taylor's secrets of decorating high fired stoneware with brightly coloured glaze effects during a reduction firing.

The fact that the same kiln and computer technology was used for both oxidised and reduction firing was an added complication. Some of the recent Ruskin-style glaze effect pieces had become increasingly interesting. To Hugh's dismay, however, Justin Emery had started to show the same reluctance to part with his glaze recipes as William Howson-Taylor had done at Ruskin Pottery 65 years earlier. His reasons were different. Justin was a perfectionist, and to release imperfect glaze recipes was not acceptable. Only fully-tested recipes should be placed in the public domain, preferably in the hands of someone who knew how to use them!

Jeanne McDougall's return to the Moorcroft fold had been a talking point at the May Open Weekend, with more than one collector commenting that the Dark Lady was in fact fair. She was also an Essex girl, Hugh reminded those who asked, as were his three daughters. From the day Jeanne was released to work at home, she vanished almost as successfully as she had done a year earlier. Hugh now had only Elise Adams with whom to share his room. Two was company, three a crowd. To ask one person to leave the room when the Chairman had something confidential to discuss was one thing. To ask two to leave was another altogether, and more often than not it was Hugh who retreated to the staff canteen to receive Moorcroft visitors.

On one of her rare visits to the Works, Jeanne produced drawings for a collection of lilies drawn on Moorcroft's 46/10 shape. Lilies were already scheduled to feature on Nicola's 1999 year plate making a further collection superfluous, Hugh told a disappointed Jeanne. The design was again too loose, he added for good measure. These things had to be said if design excellence is to be the true objective; but just as Nicola Slaney had done, Jeanne held her silence and started afresh. The first trial to emerge a week or so later was a medley of cacti drawn to the 8/6 shape. Regardless of the high quality of the design, the shape, Hugh told an even more disappointed Jeanne, was already overexposed in the Moorcroft catalogue. The two of them discussed a number of alternatives.

Eventually the designer opted for the contours of Beverley Wilkes' Meknes vase designated by Mr John as the 576/9 shape. For Hugh the collector the end result was stunning. Rich warm blues, yellows and lime green fused together as if by magic. The piece radiated colour in the way that only Jeanne could make it do; uncompromising, alive, and very American. If anything, Jeanne was more relieved than pleased, doubly so when Hugh told her that her Oranges ginger jar was controlled, tight, colourful and ready for formal design approval. The jar made his tummy turn somersaults, a sure sign that collectors would probably like it. The real conundrum was that both the ginger jar and the cactus vase could only be one-off pieces. There was no room for a further limited edition or range. What was needed was a third one-off vase to make a small trio for Jeanne in the Design Studio section of the catalogue.

Jeanne's answer was a Bird of Paradise design drawn on the delicately waisted 98/8 shape. The lines of the design were again accurate and tight, and the piece had all the excitement and charm last seen in the designer's Martinique coral reef work. The three pieces taken together would liven up the Design Studio presentation. The cactus would be Arizona, Hugh intoned solemnly. The Oranges ginger jar would be Florida and the Bird of Paradise California. At a design meeting held shortly afterwards, those present agreed. No American collector would have cause to complain about

*Arizona. Height 22 cm (9").*

Moorcroft's 1999 presentation. Although Jeanne was not to know it at the time, the very first Arizona vase now sits in pride of place in a house outside Tuscon, Arizona, taken there as a gift by a collector to an old American friend.

There was something still to come, Jeanne teased, and the very essence of the design included tight lines, she added as an afterthought. Hugh had not been prepared for such explosive output from the Design Studio's latest recruit. What emerged from the artist's case was a bright collection of hot air balloon drawings. Years before, Moorcroft had designed balloons to a charger, and Moorcroft was happy to leave it to dealers and auction houses to decide how successful or otherwise that design had been. What was now under scrutiny was a sky full of assorted balloons, all drifting serenely over a distant grey landscape below. It was different. Everything that came from Jeanne McDougall was different, and it was important for Moorcroft that she should remain different. To be different denies tradition. There was nothing 'traditional' about the design-led company Moorcroft had become.

If it was to continue to reach upwards and outwards to the highest level of the applied arts, it had to be different; it had to lead, and it could not afford to be merely traditional. It was not enough simply to try and tell the world that a particular design was brilliant. Moorcroft collectors were becoming even more perceptive. Magnolia Ivory, Violet and Bramble were already on the verge of becoming traditional, as well as tired. So too was Anemone Blue. As designs, all four had been around for a long time, Anemone Blue since 1937, and even Anemone Blue would soon have to make way for something else. Those who praised it said that Magnolia was a good starter range, but it did not follow that collectors should never be offered another design in the same price bracket to start a collection. It was beginning to look as if Emma Bossons' prototype Frangipani vases might bear witness to that.

'So what do you think of my balloons?' asked Jeanne. On offer was a radical new design in Jeanne's radical style. He had no doubt, Hugh told a relieved Jeanne, that the next design meeting would approve her balloons, but not enough work had been done. There was room for at least seven balloon pieces in the 1999 catalogue! The ultimate judges of what was both different and acceptable would be those most important of all people, the Moorcroft collectors themselves.

Meanwhile Debbie Hancock had undertaken some intricate design work for Moorcroft on *Gustavia augusta*, a flower from the Amazon rainforests. Her design

ABOVE: *Florida. Height 20 cm (8").*
BELOW: *California. Height 20 cm (8").*

*Maureen Edwards, corporate mother and publisher*

caught the eye of many Moorcroft visitors to the Works. Although almost all of them liked it, the name Gustavia Augusta sounded slightly academic. It was also difficult to remember. Drawn on a 25cm bowl as well as on the 4/8, 46/10 and 769/6 shapes, the ground colour was a sober avocado green against which had been drawn large swirling flowers with light orange centres fading to white, with a flush of subtle pink at the extremities of the petals. It was an unusually well-balanced collection, and all four pieces passed each stage of the design approval process without modification to feature in the Design Studio section of the catalogue. Sadly, no-one could come up with an alternative name.

All this frenetic activity was pre-millennium. The winds of change were blowing strongly. The year 1999 would arrive with three limited editions, a Collectors' Club vase and a year plate. There was still much design work to do. Completion of the new Nile Street factory was imminent, and a new stoneware business on the point of launch. Perhaps most important of all, the August acquisition of Kingsley Enamels had to be fitted into the Moorcroft scheme. Life was hectic for former commercial lawyer Hugh Edwards and his Moorcroft colleagues. He was supposed to be retired, and yet each day life seemed to spin faster. Curiously, total involvement at Moorcroft often had the perverse effect of denying Hugh the collector the luxury of indulging in his favourite hobby. To ensure the success of a business you love, it is necessary to give total commitment and total objectivity. For Maureen it was much the same. As a mother of four herself, she loved children of all ages. To set up and run a factory crèche is not an endless stream of baby cuddles, but a job involving stringent legislative compliance obligations, thorough vetting of staff and procedures to deal with each crisis as it arises.

For Hugh, there was no time to worry about how Sweet Briar might be represented in 1999 following the pricing fiasco a year earlier. Nicola Slaney had

*Balloons. Tallest Vase 25cm (10").*

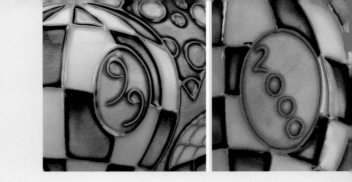

started work on a massive design for the millennium, tentatively called Jerusalem; but the operative word was 'started'. Even the shape of the vase was undecided. As was his habit, Hugh had tried not to put pressure on either Nicola or Emma to come forward with ideas based on their experience in the South Pacific. Emma had already produced two of the three limited editions for 1999, and because of that and a variety of other reasons Hugh had no doubt that the millennium presentation would all come together somehow.

To alleviate pressure on the Moorcroft Chairman's time, positive action had been taken to take away some of his work load. Kim Thompson, Keith Dawson and Steven Swann had all been made directors of Cobridge Stoneware. More significantly, on 1 October, Ted Turner started work at Moorcroft as finance director. On the same day, the hugely popular, hard-working and effective Keith Dawson was promoted to production director at Moorcroft.

On 10 September the contractors finally vacated the new Nile Street factory, leaving behind them the usual 'snagging lists' itemising remedial work, including a car park surface that was already breaking up and in need of renewal. The development of the Nile Street site for Cobridge Stoneware had not been an edifying experience. In total contrast, the opening ceremony at the Phoenix Works on 16 September 1998 was an historic occasion to savour and remember. Government Minister Richard Caborn MP cut the red tape jointly with the 99.5 year old Patty Booth, a former decorator at Moorcroft. Joan Walley, the Cobridge Member of Parliament, was there too, and it was Joan who pushed Patty's wheelchair all the way from the Moorcroft factory in Sandbach Road across Cobridge Park to the new Phoenix Works.

It was a moving experience for the hundreds of people who turned out to watch. Patty was the sole survivor of the line of pottery workers who had walked crocodile from the old James Macintyre factory to the Moorcroft Factory in 1912. This time she led the new workforce back again, almost a hundred of them, her chair pushed by an MP and a senior Government Minister. Behind her came the placers, the turners, the decorators, sgraffitoers, tube-liners, the warehouse staff and selectors, the claymen and the mould-makers all carrying their equipment and tools of their trade as their predecessors had done more than eighty four years earlier. The nursery staff were there too, plus babies and toys. Inside, Hugh could have wept. It was an emotional, moving and colourful sight all at the same time. A hundred new jobs in a depressed inner city area walking together to a new workplace.

*Gustavia Augusta. Tallest Vase 25 cm (10").*

Nothing ever happens in this world unless you make it happen. From the new staff canteen with its curved windows at first floor level, Minister Richard Caborn pointed out to Hugh the derelict site on the opposite side of Nile Street, with its asbestos sheds the size of aeroplane hangars, rusty old barrels, broken glass and barbed wire, concrete and disused mineshafts. It was, the Minister said, what his job was all about, and he spent the next five minutes telling the Moorcroft chairman of his own ambitions for inner-city regeneration. Five months later, Moorcroft acquired that three-acre site for a second new factory.

Despite the work-load, it was fun. New faces and old faces were enjoying their work together. Even the regular malfunction of the huge, computer-controlled stoneware gas kiln in Nile Street failed to dampen the enthusiasm that percolated into every corner of the Moorcroft workforce during those dramatic months making up a wet and cold autumn and winter. Hugh's depression had completely vanished. Whichever way he looked at it, the summer of 1998, despite its dramas and delays, had turned into one of the happiest times of his life. Collectors came in increasing numbers to the factory shop, not necessarily to buy, but to absorb the atmosphere of a company forging its own destiny as it moved steadily towards the millennium. If it touches you even lightly, Moorcroft's art can become all-absorbing. It seduces you into another world, where the only purpose is the pursuit of excellence and where the ultimate goal is total satisfaction for those involved in the experience. There were times, Hugh remarked to a startled Elise Adams, when the only thing to do was to dance and sing!

*Patty Booth cutting the tape at the opening of the Phoenix Works, Nile Street, jointly with the Rt. Hon. Richard Caborn MP*

# FOURTEEN

# Happy Landing

Photography had always fascinated Hugh and Maureen. Neither was a particularly good photographer, but both recognised that images, special moments of time, passing wonders of life, often flashed by so quickly that only the split-second timing of the camera could encapsulate those events for ever. When Emma and Nicola showed the two of them some of their favourite photographs taken during their visit to the South Pacific, Hugh and Maureen allowed themselves the luxury of reliving with the designers highlights of their visit. There was a beautiful pink orchid, *Catleya mandelii*, which Nicola had found in Fiji's Garden of the Sleeping Giant, a treasure trove collection of literally thousands of stunningly beautiful orchids from all over the world put together by the late Raymond Burr, better known for his television role as Perry Mason.

A few days earlier, the two intrepid designer-explorers had taken a plane to the outlying Fijian island of Tavouni where Emma's restless camera had snapped up the sensitive plant, so called because of its habit of furling its leaves when touched. She had also taken great care to photograph every kind of frangipani flower she could find, while at the same time absorbing other images of white sand, coconut palms and a turquoise sea. Through the designers' album of photographic records, the Edwards were able to re-visit the volcanic island of Rarotonga, its rugged mountains shrouded semi-permanently in a dark mist which swirled mysteriously around the volcanic peaks as if trying to obliterate all memories of human sacrifice and cannibalism practised there right through to the twentieth century. Hugh shivered. In the year 2000, he would be able to describe those events as taking place during the last century. It would feel safer in design terms that way!

Tahiti was an island of dreams – warm, humid and with a faint smell of perfume in the air. On their higher slopes, the mountains were covered with rainforest, while further down nearer the coast frangipani trees grew in profusion.

Emma had taken to frangipani flowers in a big way, whereas Nicola had fallen in love with the perfume tree. No wonder Fletcher Christian and his Bounty mutineers had settled on the island with its lush vegetation, coffee-coloured friendly people, music and dance.

*Emma and Nicola with their Dateline series*
Photograph courtesy of Collect-It! magazine

Neither designer said much about Rarotonga. The Edwards assumed, incorrectly, that this had something to do with the island's troubled and often violent history. The truth was rather more simple. One night after a solid day's walking, climbing and sketching, both girls decided they were ready for an early night. Nicola was first into bed and lay looking at the ceiling. Suddenly she screamed and fled to the bathroom, slamming the door shut behind her. As she did so, Emma, who was about to climb into bed herself, was conscious of something 'vaguely green' falling from the ceiling between the girls' beds.

Cautiously, and some would say bravely, the youngest member of the Moorcroft Design Studio knelt down on the floor and peered under Nicola's bed. What she saw was a large green and red lizard. At that, she too screamed loud and long, causing the lizard to scurry under a chest of drawers. In the absence of anyone on call to remove the terrified reptile, both designers spent an uncomfortable night in the bathroom with a towel under the door, Emma in the bath tub itself and Nicola huddled up under the washbasin. The whole experience impressed itself deeply into their minds. To the sound of croaking bull frogs and the distant clatter of a noisy swamp hen, inspiration took hold of both of them. From Emma came Lizzie, the Rarotonga lizard, and from Nicola came the colourful Swamp Hen. The bull frogs have yet to appear.

Kiribati was different. Pronounced Kiribass, the former Gilbert Islands have little to offer travellers except coconut palms, white coral sand and turquoise lagoons. The Edwards could still remember taking their family to what was probably the most remote collection of atolls on God's earth. It was a place to lie in a hammock and let the equatorial breezes waft gently across your face or watch the

FACING: *Pacific Island Paradise*

local fishermen work the lagoon with their lines, nets and spears. Houses were built precariously on wooden stilts and thatched with pandanus leaves. Only the sound of the occasional pig snuffling among the coconut husks broke the interminable roar of the surf beyond the distant coral reefs. Emma's first trials of her Kiribati design showed a hammock swinging lazily between two coconut palms while a small canoe bobbed on the blue waters of the lagoon. Without much prompting Emma removed the hammock and the canoe on her second trial, and for the Edwards as one-time visitors to the islands, the piece was perfect. Kiribati was as near to heaven on earth as even the most hardened traveller could expect to find. At a design meeting on 21 October everyone present agreed.

Emma asked Hugh which of her two Sensitive Plant trials he liked the best. The design on each was the same, a delicate combination of flower heads with small, fernlike leaves growing from stems which wound up organically from the base of the pot to the rim. The designer had selected the 99/8 shape, last used by Rachel Bishop for her Phoenix Bird vase, Moorcroft's best-selling piece of all time. Hugh's personal favourite was the version painted against a soft mustard ground which faded into a brownish green at the base and rim. Emma screwed up her nose, the young designer's way of showing that she disagreed. Her own favourite was the alternative vase with its cool green-gold ground and purple flower heads, all cleverly finished with a dark moss colour at base and rim.

There was not much to choose between them, but enough, Hugh initially thought, to fight for the mustard version at the next design meeting. Emma looked unhappy, as if she were reading his thoughts. That look lingered in his mind, and when the time arrived Hugh backed his designer speaking in favour of her green Sensitive Plant. The vase was approved for production, as were Nicola's Orchid on the 101/7 vase, her Swamp Hen ginger jar and Perfume Tree on the 32/8 shape. Whenever a new design is brought forward for approval at a design meeting, no decision is ever made about the future use of each approved design. That is decided later in the privacy of a formal Board meeting in the absence of the designers.

With images of New Zealand in her mind, Emma had also worked up a striking orchid design of her own on the 93/12 shape – the Edwardian vase, as Hugh preferred to call it. Soft pink orchid flowers nestled against a washed grey ground. At its base the woodsmoke grey was almost black, but faded to a very light grey towards the rim. To have two pink orchid vases in the same design presentation troubled Hugh. Additionally, Nicola's orchid had been drawn on the same shape as Debbie Hancock's Convolvulus design introduced to collectors during Moorcroft's Open Weekend earlier in the year. That clinched the matter. To produce two pieces on the same shape within such a short period of time would be unwise. Because of the earlier exposure of the shape of vase itself, Emma's pink orchid was more likely to be the preferred candidate at the next design meeting. Even so, the orchid on Emma's vase was somehow just a little too pink. After canvassing opinion about the Works, the designer concluded that the crown or lip of the top orchids on the vase should be purple with a strong yellow centre and not just plain pink. That revision was a great improvement, and together with Lizzie on its tiny 2/4 shape, Emma's Orchid was ready for final trials.

It was an open secret at the Works that the Slaney/Bossons Dateline Series would comprise six pieces. Everyone felt that six pieces was the correct number to introduce to collectors to represent Moorcroft at the millennium. Included in the six pieces would be the Birth of Light plate as the anchor design. It was never suggested that the plate should be produced in an edition of two thousand. That was an assumption made by all concerned, and it was an assumption which remained unchallenged until the day the first approved pieces emerged from the kiln. The trouble was that even discounting the plate, the Moorcroft Board had seven designs approved for production of which only five were needed to complete the Dateline Series.

After considerable discussion and many expressions of glee at having a selection from which to choose, the Board decided to drop Nicola Slaney's Swamp Hen ginger jar on the ground that the base colour replicated the base colour used by Wendy Mason on the millennium plate. Also taken out of consideration was Nicola's piece inspired by the pink orchid *Cattleya mandelii*. The Board's reasoning was simple. The colour impact of the piece was not dissimilar to Emma's orchid, and more importantly the 101/7 shape had been used during the previous Open Weekend. As a small consolation, Nicola's Serviceberry design, inspired by *Amelanchier laevis*, was approved for production, although not on the 65/6 shape which the designer had used as a trial. The 65/6 vase was already in use for Spike, the Collectors' Day piece for 1998. A different shape would be required.

Inadequate designers will pout, stamp their feet, act petulant and even sulk when faced with rejection. The remarkable fact about the Moorcroft Design Studio was that this never happened. Admittedly most, but by no means all, designs brought forward by the designers for approval had gone on into production in one way or another. Emma's Hellebore had failed to find a slot in the millenni-

um catalogue but on the narrow ground that her friend Nicola's Hellebore duplicated her own. It was Nicola's design that was selected, largely because it had
a more 'organic' feel, but that was all. No one bothered much – not even Emma
herself. Great designers move on, whatever reverses they face, restlessly seeking
higher levels of achievement.

Hugh was not surprised when Nicola Slaney called in to see him to say that
her Jerusalem drawings for a massive prestige vase to represent Moorcroft at the
millennium were coming on well. Then find time to design a millennium range
or two as well, the Moorcroft Chairman replied with a smile. He sensed that
Nicola would pick up the challenge, and that it was only a question of when.
A second look at Nicola's lily design on the 1999 Year Plate would be as good a
starting point as any, Hugh suggested.

A fax from Moorcroft's Australian distributor, Philip Allen, lay unanswered
on the shelf beside Hugh's desk. It was now time for Moorcroft to consider its
Australian and New Zealand collectors once more. Philip has asked for a piece
with an Australian floral design exclusively for the Australian market. Over the
past twelve years similar requests had resulted in Wattle Banksia, Tall Ships
(HMS Sirius), Blue Gum and the colourful Sulphur Crested Cockatoo. If Hugh
was to respond to Philip Allen's fax in a positive way, a designer had to be identified to create a suitable design and almost certainly travel to the Antipodes.

The Design Studio's youngest member, Emma Bossons, had made a significant contribution to Moorcroft's millennium design presentation. So too had
Nicola Slaney. It was also important to remember that Elise Adams had exceeded all expectations as Collectors' Club Secretary and, more importantly, she was
happy to take a front-line role attending Collectors' Days. As a result she too had
a claim to travel in her own right. Any residual doubts that Hugh may have had
about Elise's strength of character and commitment to Moorcroft's collectors
evaporated one Saturday in late October. The occasion had been the launch of
Underwood, the special limited edition vase designed by Debbie Hancock exclusively for James Macintyre. From the moment he met up with Elise in Leeds' Victoria Quarter, Hugh felt instinctively that something was seriously wrong.

Elise's answer to his question was straight to the point. Her father was criti-
cally ill in Wrexham hospital. Offering his car to Moorcroft sales manager Steven
Swann, who had driven to Leeds in a van, Hugh asked him to take Elise directly
to her father in hospital. He would take the van back to Stoke on Trent himself.
Early the following day, Elise's father died, but not before saying goodbye to his

*Dateline Series. Tallest vase 30 cm (12"). From top clockwise: Tahiti, Aotearoa, Fiji, Kiribati, Rarotonga
and Birth of Light millennium plate.*

daughter. Three days later, she crashed her car. To the joy and surprise of all her colleagues at Moorcroft, Elise presented herself for work the following Monday. 'Better to work, Boss,' she joked, 'than sit miserable at home.' Hugh responded instinctively, and gave the Collectors' Club Secretary a large hug!

At the works, plans for the millennium trip to the Antipodes started to mature. Philip Allen was cool on an attendance by the Collectors' Club Secretary. His preference was for a double designer visit with its enhanced potential for media interest. Reluctantly Hugh found himself agreeing, largely because Emma Bossons was the prime candidate and Emma's alternative travelling companion was likely to be Nicola, both of whom had already experienced time away together in the South Pacific. And so it was. The two young designers would be attractive ambassadors for Moorcroft. Emma was ready to take on the responsibility, and with Nicola at her elbow she would have close and continuous support. Both jumped at the proposal once again, and with faultless timing Hugh asked Emma to consider creating a special pair of vases for Philip Allen to consider. Because Philip had specifically requested a floral design with an overt Australian theme. Emma's response was the Sturt Desert Pea, state flower of South Australia.

Both of the first Sturt Desert Pea trials were exquisite. The larger vase was drawn for the 62/7 shape, and the smaller to the 35/3 shape. As far as Hugh was concerned, Australian distributor Philip Allen ought to be pleased. September 1999 was pencilled into the diaries of those concerned as a possible month for the trip. There was plenty of time for Hugh to work out the full details when Philip Allen came to the United Kingdom to attend the 1999 Birmingham International Spring Fair.

Apart from the millennium plate itself, names for the Dateline series designs were still to be finalised. Hugh knew that New Zealand would be one of the first countries on earth to see in the millennium. A fax to Robert Denning-Kemp, Moorcroft's distributor in New Zealand, established that the Maori name for New Zealand was Aotearoa which translated as 'the land of the long white cloud'. That was it! Emma's 30cm Orchid vase would be called Aotearoa, while her Sensitive Plant from Tavouni would be called after Tavouni's mother island, Fiji. The simplicity of the coconut palms shading the white coral shores of Kiribati's islands convinced everyone that Emma's superb design of an equatorial atoll should be called Kiribati. Tahiti would provide the name for Nicola's Perfume Tree, while Emma's mischievous lizard would be known as Rarotonga forever. At

FACING: *Sturt Desert Pea, final vases on the 62/11 and 226/7 shapes. Tall vase 27 cm (11").*

this stage, an inquisitive collector might be tempted to ask about the fate of Nicola Slaney's Pink Orchid, Swamp Hen and Indian Summer – the latter approved several weeks earlier on the ever popular 7/5 shape. As in all of these things, Hugh's thought processes had already moved forward to November 1998. He was an incorrigible collector, and because of that, November was likely to be a month which included rather more than just Bonfire Night.

# FIFTEEN

# Getting in Shape

It would have been understandable if Rachel had been disappointed to see her Passion Fruit range fade out after just one year, or her Poppy range cut in two for the 1999 catalogue presentation; but something really exciting from Moorcroft's senior designer was already waiting in the wings to take their place. It was Islay, and after only a handful of minor amendments, made shortly after the end of Rachel's maternity leave, the Islay design settled down comfortably in the Design Studio section of the catalogue on the 4/8, 869/9$^{1}/_{2}$, 7/7 and 198/5 shapes, all of which doubled as lamps. Rachel's first Islay design had shown a straight shoreline, but the final, crucial alteration involved the creation of a salt water loch which meandered into the distance. It was not hard to imagine the crunching sound of dry sand underfoot or the tang of salt in the air, the sound of wheeling, screaming gulls and the sweet smell of heather all coming together in a glorious celebration of open space and freedom. This was the real Islay, the island of dreams, of Gallic plainsong, storytelling and whisky.

Rachel had also worked her magic on Oberon. Her successful range had been freshened with the inclusion of two new shapes, while three other shapes exited the catalogue to compensate. Lamia had received similar Bishop treatment with three new shapes added to the range and four leaving it. To the casual observer, this might seem to have been nothing more than pure artistic mechanics. The reality is different. Shape changes are as important as design changes to a collector who will readily understand why Moorcroft's Tribute to Charles Rennie Mackintosh range was so strengthened by the inclusion of two new shapes. From the day she first arrived at Moorcroft, Rachel had made it clear that she liked to keep all ranges moving forward, eliminating less successful shapes and inserting new ones in their place. In this way, she makes sure that nothing ever stands still. Collectors' interest is maintained, and designs remain as fresh and interesting as when first conceived.

While the process of refreshing ranges moved forward, it was Kim Thompson who noticed that one range had actually moved backwards. Sweet Briar had been mis-priced months earlier and from that moment on the design all but died. In what seemed to be no time at all, Rachel again worked her magic. To replace the hapless 62/7 and 99/8 shapes, the senior designer introduced a clock plus four vases on the 364/5, 80/6, 7/7, 92/11 and 849/8 shapes to complete a new Sweet Briar presentation for 1999.

*Islay. Height 20 cm (8").*

The Design Studio had been created in the middle of 1997. Thereafter, its composition and purpose had been planned over a period of several months. By the end of 1998, there was every indication it was settling down to an extended future far beyond the year 2000. Detractors would continue to mouth objections, or quietly suggest there was no need to dispense with the old single designer philosophy, or to change a system which had worked for better or for worse over more than a hundred years. Deep down, this criticism overlooked two important points. The first was the burden of contemporary design requirements at Moorcroft. If insufficient designs were created to meet collectors' expectations, Moorcroft might rapidly reverse its present strong and colourful progress, and slide back into oblivion. What had been enough to sustain survival even three years earlier was not enough to sustain survival past the millennium.

The second more subtle reason was that both William and Walter Moorcroft had been proprietors of the business for which they designed. The notion of either of them moving away to work elsewhere was not a serious proposition. Admittedly, William had to report to Liberty as a pre-condition to collecting his salary cheque, but he also had an equity stake in Moorcroft. That was a serious and compelling reason for him to stay. None of the present Design Studio members owned shares in Moorcroft. Good pay, a generous pension scheme and good working conditions, matched with full credit for all creative success, was only a partial means of securing Design Studio loyalty.

The more successful the Design Studio became the greater the necessity to ensure that all its members felt a strong involvement in Moorcroft and its art. Design is the lifeblood of Moorcroft, running as it does through the very heart of the

FACING: *Islay. Tallest vase 24 cm. (9½").*

company. One day designers and indeed all other members of the Moorcroft workforce would be given the opportunity to own shares in their company. To secure its long-term survival there was a strong argument that Moorcroft should be owned and managed by those who committed their lives to the company.

To run a business you love is a joy. To be involved in Moorcroft as a collector can be a distraction. Those who subscribe to this simple truth will understand why it was that during the late summer, Hugh found himself delving into dusty 'carry-care' trays in the Moorcroft cellars looking at discarded pots. To be fair, the arrival of the 1998 Christmas season was uppermost in his mind. There were a number of unwanted trial pieces lying around gathering dust on the hard, iron shelves – not to mention a handful of very attractive dated pieces. Only a few days earlier Hugh had unearthed a box containing some twenty superb trials of small Ryden Lane vases. Some were more blue at the base and the neck than the original limited edition vase, but all had a range of colours in the flower heads and leaves varying from a gentle yellow to rich purple. A few really special pieces had cow parsley heads which were almost iridescent pink.

The Ryden Lane trials had come into existence after Rachel's decision to re-work her original design onto a number of small and medium-sized shapes, each carrying a subtle variation of the original design theme. Everyone loved them, but the Ryden Lane design involved complex tube-lining. That on its own would not have been enough to prevent the vases coming through for production as a range, as had already happened once in the past with Carp. The deciding factor against the range idea was that the original RM3/27 limited edition vase was scheduled to continue in production until the end of 1999. To run the large vase in tandem with a new range of smaller pieces would have been unwise, and the Ryden Lane trials had been consigned to the cellar as a result.

In September 1998, and quite independently, Mr John had suggested a radical re-appraisal of the Moorcroft Museum display. There were too many exhibits stored away in locked cupboards, calling for a decision on the possible disposal of surplus pieces. In a strange way, that single suggestion was the catalyst which lead directly to a new event for Moorcroft collectors. The idea was that the whole of the month of November would contain a special Moorcroft promotion in the factory shop, culminating in a first-ever Collectors' Christmas party over the last weekend of the month. It would be a one-off chance for collectors to mix together and swap stories about the preceding year, to share mince pies and mulled wine, to buy trials and Moorcroft's rare dated pieces, not to mention the surplus

FACING: Top right and left. Sweet Briar. Tallest vase 27 cm (11").
Bottom left: Lamia. Tallest vase 20 cm (8").
Bottom Right: Tribute to Charles Rennie Mackintosh. Tall vase 22 cm (9").

*Ryden Lane artwork for smaller pieces (above) and trials (facng). Tallest vase 25 cm (10″).*

museum exhibits identified by Mr John. Every collector would be invited.

Several years earlier, Moorcroft had locked horns with the Inland Revenue when the Revenue tried to assert that the Moorcroft Museum Collection was in fact old stock, and should be taken into account in assessing company profits. The fact that many pieces had lain hidden in boxes in the factory cellars buried under several centimetres of soot from Moorcroft's original five kilns was neither here nor there as far as the Revenue were concerned. Each piece, said the tax man, had been made by Moorcroft at the Works and because it remained unsold, it was stock. Almost 80 years had passed since many of pieces had been fired, but that was not an argument which impressed the Revenue at all. Stock was stock, however old. The real sting in the tail was the assertion that the stock should be valued at current market value rather than the last ex-works price for each piece!

Moorcroft fought the Inland Revenue and Moorcroft won. With help from Hugh's former colleagues at Richards Butler, the company successfully proved that the Museum exhibits had been taken out of the 'income' net and designated as 'capital' many years earlier without objection. Because the Inland Revenue had been unable to identify which pieces of 'old' Moorcroft had been swept up by a single, all-embracing 1983 entry of £20,069 in the company's accounts, they were forced to concede that all old pieces about the Works at the time were included in the £20,069 figure. With that, their claim for the most part disintegrated. Even so, fearing a programme of disposals of what they still saw as stock, the Revenue asked for and obtained from Moorcroft a formal undertaking not to dispose of Museum exhibits, whether on show or not, until more than twelve months had elapsed after the date of discontinuation of the legal action. That twelve-month period had long since expired, and who better to buy ex-Museum pieces than Moorcroft collectors themselves?

By the time November arrived, the Design Studio had been commissioned for the first time to produce special pieces for the event. Most of them were already working long hours for Kingsley Enamels, and the extra burden inevitably intruded into their free time. Keith Dawson had no gaps in his pre-Christmas production schedule to make special pieces, and the only available option was to invite decorators and tube-liners to undertake a complex overtime schedule to convert the extra work done by the Design Studio into Moorcroft pottery. Each tube-liner/decorator team was lead by a designer. Hugh and Keith also devised a scheme for each of the designer-led teams which yielded a profit-share of 12$\frac{1}{2}$ calculated on the retail price of every special piece sold from the factory shop during November. In turn, it was agreed that the commission would be divided among each team in such proportions agreed among themselves. Moorcroft would pay basic rates for all overtime hours worked. The 12½ per cent pool was an additional bonus from which only the necessary statutory deductions would be made.

The designers were quick and positive in their response, despite their tiredness and workload. Nicola offered a pretty Christmas Rose vase and plate, while her friend Emma weighed in with a Christmas Carnation jug in two slightly different colourways. Angela Davenport produced Samburu Giraffes, one 'daytime' and one 'evening' piece on the 159/10 shape, plus a handful of tiny Hummingbird pieces. One or two hummingbirds had been enriched with a subtle golden lustre on their wings, which Keith had personally applied before a third firing, after talking it through with Angela. From their 'carry-tray' in the cellar, the rare Ryden Lane trials on small vases also emerged for the occasion, to be snapped up by an enthusiastic collecting public.

Debbie Hancock's Camellia on the 4/8 shape, and Angela Davenport's Mandeville on the tiny 46/4 shape arrived in a number of colourways, as

*Christmas Rose. Vase 17 cm (7″) high.*

did Shirley Hayes' Malvia design on the 8/6 vase. Shirley had only recently joined the Design Studio, largely on the recommendation of other members. The star turns, however, were the three limited edition pieces, all designed by Nicola Slaney. Her Swamp Hen ginger jar came in an edition of 50; the Pink Orchid on the 101/7 shape in an edition limited to 100; and Indian Summer on the 7/5 shape in an edition limited to 50. By popular acclaim, the favourite was Nicola's Swamp Hen. It was not hard to imagine the sound of its chatter as it waded through its marsh homeland on the South Pacific island of Rarotonga.

By the end of November, old trials had been cleaned and polished; further exquisite dated pieces were unearthed from a corner of Moorcroft's damp and airless cellar, while the special pieces designed and made for the November party sparkled in all their colourful beauty on the glass shelves in the factory shop. Day

one of Collectors' Christmas Weekend was sheer good-natured pandemonium. Visitors moved with impressive skill among the pieces on offer. It was one of those times where the old collector's adage 'never put it down unless you have decided against it' was more than apt.

After the last collector had disappeared into the November night, Kim Thompson was heard to remark that for the first time in Moorcroft's history, success could be measured by the number of mince pies consumed by collectors in just one weekend. With well over 2,000 to be paid for, not to mention enough mulled wine to start an off-licence, finance director Ted Turner's views on the likes and dislikes of the Moorcroft Collectors' Club underwent a radical change. The November celebration was seen as a huge success, with Collectors' Club Secretary Elise Adams inundated with letters and phone calls requesting a repeat in 1999. Keith was apprehensive. November 1999 was just one month away from the millennium, but Elise aligned herself against him. As Collectors' Club Secretary it was her job to ensure that the silent army of Moorcroft collectors were not forgotten, and this included their aspirations for the eve of the millennium. In his own corner, Hugh had not forgotten the vases still missing from his list of designs required to greet the year 2000. One of the most important was a Collectors' Day piece for retailers hosting Moorcroft's Collectors' Days during 1999, as well as a May Open Weekend vase for the same year.

Mince pies and mulled wine apart, by the end of the month many of the designers, tube-liners and decorators had gone beyond tiredness and, as one of them said, into autodrive. Some worked until seven each evening; others gave up their free Friday afternoons or evenings; and some even worked on Saturdays. It was Angela Davenport who pointed out shortly before

ABOVE: *Christmas Carnation.* Height of jug 24 cm (9½"). BELOW: *Pink Orchid, Indian Summer* and *Swamp Hen.* Height of ginger jar 15 cm (6").

FACING: *Top left: Samburu Giraffes 25 cm (10"). Top right: Hummingbird and Mandeville (centre back) 10 cm (4"). Bottom left: Camellia 20cm (8"). Bottom right: Malvia 1cm (6")*

Christmas that one group had worked continuously throughout all available overtime slots! Heavy eyelids and yawns certainly, but it was a wonderful response to receive from the Moorcroft workforce, all the more so because best quality stock continued to be dispatched in record quantities to the company's retail partners throughout November. Nobody was a loser.

While finance director Ted Turner all but wept over the size of some of the team's salary cheques, collectors were given a feast of special designs in addition to the usual trials and Moorcroft's special dated pieces. What was most noticeable of all was just how responsive everyone was to Keith Dawson. Soon after his arrival at Moorcroft, he would often be seen sitting with those working in the decorating shop listening, coaxing, praising and occasionally cajoling gently. It was as if Keith belonged to them, understood their anxieties and aspirations. He was a man who saw it as his duty to serve his workforce rather than adopt the old imperial 'stick and carrot' method so common in the Potteries, where tradition ruled with an iron rod.

In a company with little hierarchical structure, where people work together

on first-name terms, sharing with each other both pain and laughter, Keith fitted into things as if he had been there forever. One day soon Mr John would retire, and on that day, if not before, the rumour was that Moorcroft would put Keith into the British Ceramic Confederation in his place. If that happened, the Moorcroft production director would arrive with the force of a typhoon, bringing with him the Moorcroft philosophies on management style. To serve your workforce properly as a director involves sheer hard work and total honesty: no afternoon rounds of golf or lunch at the Potters Club; no middle-aged executives holding pots or glass to create the illusion that in some important way they had been involved in their creation. Among many other things, Keith objected to management stealing their workforce's credits. Moorcroft's record pre-Christmas despatch to its retailers saw Keith out of bed at 5.30 am, preparing the Works for the day ahead by 6.30 am, and home for supper by 9 pm at night, if he was lucky. Keith practised what he preached. Hugh admired him for it.

*Samarkand Lily. Height 17 cm (7").*

His colleagues loved him for it.

Since late summer 1998, Debbie Hancock had been working on an unusual design featuring flowers that were almost electric blue, each set against a surprisingly warm orange/brown ground. The first trial, on the 101/7 shape, was dismissed out of hand at a design meeting for the very real reason that the 101/7 was the same shape used by Debbie for her successful Convolvulus vase sold during Open Weekend a year earlier. A repeat would be premature. Her second trial appeared on the 364/8 shape. It was attractive, certainly, but still failed to provoke that special feeling of magic which comes only when shape and design work together in total harmony. Debbie Hancock, a designer never known to acknowledge a setback, commissioned a completely new vase shape and started designing once more. This time design and shape dovetailed, and the piece was passed for production. Called Samarkand Lily, the new shape was recorded as the 226/7 by Mr John. Samarkand Lily would

*Serviceberry. Height 12 cm (5").*

be the first piece to run as a limited edition at Open Weekend, and after discussion it was agreed that the number of vases made would be limited to 250.

A similar story attached itself to Nicola Slaney's delicate Serviceberry, initially designed for the 198/5 shape. The first trial had fallen short of Nicola's increasingly high standards for a number of reasons, and she took the decision to revisit her choice of shape as well as implement a few alterations. However, as occasionally happens in the life of an art pottery, other matters intervened. On this occasion, it was Alan Wright, master salesman second to none, and the Edwards' most loyal friend at Moorcroft, plus a shareholder for good measure. Alan had received a semi-official proposal from a government-backed company seeking top quality ceramics to exhibit in the Millennium Dome in Greenwich. There was something vague about the proposal which worried Hugh, a feeling that increased when he discovered that the sole shareholder of the company was Peter Mandelson, the former Secretary of State for Trade and Industry.

What had been requested through Alan Wright was an exclusive design, probably a limited edition, to be sold directly from the Millennium Dome. The proposal would be a further incursion into design time already in short supply, but as a potentially prestigious assignment it was a challenge worth taking on.

Shortly afterwards, Nicola and Emma were introduced to John Massey of Ashwood Nurseries, a long-standing Moorcroft customer. For some time past Hugh had steered clear of direct personal involvement with Ashwood Nurseries, largely as a result of their apparent commitment to selling antiques in addition to contemporary applied arts. Antiques brought with them the unwelcome possibility of dealers emerging from the nursery compost, so Hugh had kept his distance. In the event, however, it all blew over after Ashwood were burgled and a substantial quantity of their antiques stolen. With the burglary, the Nursery's enthusiasm for buying and selling antiques rapidly diminished. Out of this stroke of bad luck, new possibilities emerged to strengthen links with Moorcroft.

On arrival at Ashwood, Hugh and the two Moorcroft designers were treated to an excellent lunch, after which Nicola and Emma were given unrestricted access to probably the most famous Hellebore greenhouse in the world. John Massey was in good form, having just won his 21st Gold Medal at the Royal Horticultural Society show a few days earlier. Sketch books, note pads and cameras were all active in the interest of a good Millennium Dome design. Before dark, both designers travelled home with some rare and colourful Hellebores of the potted kind, as well as several rolls of exposed film, notes and sketches. Emma started work almost immediately on both a Hellebore design and an extremely attractive Hepatica, another Ashwood Nursery speciality. For her own part, Nicola decided to commit herself to the 92/11 shape and create a Hellebore design herself, but nothing else. She was already wrestling with her vast Jerusalem vase, and to expect anything more from her would have been unreasonable. Design work on the 'green' Jerusalem vase had taken sixteen weeks out of her life already, and that was before the question of colour was even considered.

It thus came as an especially pleasant surprise when Hugh found himself face to face with Nicola's Serviceberry design, re-drawn and fired onto the 102/5 shape. In one move, the young designer had completed Moorcroft's outstanding design requirement for 1999 – until, that is, Kim Thompson remembered that during the November Collectors' Christmas Weekend, almost all trials and Moorcroft's special dated pieces had been sold from the company's shelves of experimental pottery. As Hugh was Moorcroft's link to the Design Studio, Kim asked him what he proposed to do about it. Collectors would have expectations for Open Weekend. They always did, but the designers were tired and already fully committed to an on-going work programme.

At that moment, Hugh remembered Emma Bossons' first Spiraxia trial on the 7/7 shape. With the recollection came an idea for Open Weekend which would deliver to collectors something even more interesting than an auction of trials: specially designed pieces from the Moorcroft workforce and the new Open Weekend limited edition piece itself. It was time for Moorcroft quietly to change the Open Weekend format. With help from the Design Studio, something new and exciting would be added to the usual treats in store for collectors.

*Nicola Slaney working on her Jerusalem vase*

# SIXTEEN

# Moorcroft Grows Small

In business, success can erupt in one place and not in another without any apparent reason. Reasons are sought but often hard to find, particularly in the precarious and unorthodox world of the applied arts. Although Elliot Hall's catalogue for Moorcroft Enamels threatened to be late, it was certainly not his fault. Between the date of the Moorcroft acquisition of his family company in August 1998 and January 1999, the twenty-five year old managing director had not only moved his factory from Bromsgrove to Worcester, but had also recruited enough artists schooled in Worcester's traditions of excellence to double his existing workforce. Although he was not to know it at the time, by the end of March the number of artists painting Moorcroft Enamels at Worcester would double yet again, so great was the demand for their work.

In Elliot Hall, Hugh saw echoes of himself. Both came from Worcestershire, as did their wives. Louise Hall had taken a good degree in Business Studies, and after passing her Banker's examinations had quickly moved on to become one of the Nationwide Building Society's youngest branch managers at the age of 25. Although a generation separated the two couples, their grass roots were very similar. Elliot Hall lived and breathed decorated enamels; they were in his blood. For Hugh, art pottery had an equally powerful attraction. To succeed in business, there is no alternative to a twenty-four hour day, seven-day week emotional commitment, sometimes little short of obsession. Nothing else works. Distant horizons, future ambitions all have to be identified, developed and achieved. Nothing in this world happens unless you make it happen.

This had always been Hugh's philosophy, and much of it was already attaching itself to Elliot. Sometimes extraneous factors intervene such as lack of support or skill, lack of money, detractors, traditionalists and pessimists. In the case of Elliot's 1999 catalogue, it was an overworked Design Studio which caused the delay. As with all good businessmen, Elliot Hall made virtue out of necessity.

FACING: *Moorcroft Enamels at the House of Lords*

While the Moorcroft Design Studio laboured on, Elliot identified sixty retailers across the British Isles as potential stockists of Moorcroft Enamels. Traditional retailers would be nervous at handling his Lilliputian range of ginger jars, vases and enamel boxes, all of them covered in new Moorcroft designs and carrying Moorcroft marks. Traditionalists always feel insecure when the winds of change start blowing.

Working with Elliot, Alan Wright and the Moorcroft sales team cross-referenced all Moorcroft artware products to see which retailers carried, or were prepared to carry, Okra Glass, Cobridge Stoneware and Moorcroft Enamels, in addition to Moorcroft pottery itself. At the same time, all existing unfulfilled orders for Moorcroft pottery on retailers' books were edited. By cutting out dead wood, retailers were able to create space in their allocation of Moorcroft pottery, and all were then free to stock up with new 1999 designs. As it turned out, there were many more retailers willing to take on Moorcroft Enamels than the sixty first identified. But sixty was a good round number, and the Moorcroft Board backed the wishes of its youngest member. Even so, Elliot and the Moorcroft team viewed the February opening of the 1999 International Spring Fair at Birmingham with some trepidation. There were now four Moorcroft group stands to think about, in stark contrast to the single stand which had proudly carried the company's centennial emblems back in 1997. The Moorcroft corporate pole had become a pyramid; four companies now constituted its base rather than one.

In twelve weeks, starting in September 1998, the Moorcroft Design Studio created an incredible eighty new designs for Elliot Hall's enamels company. The quality was so impressive that Mr John was heard to comment that his father, William, would have been pleased to see the companion designs on offer to the world alongside his own Pomegranate, Pansy, Spanish and Moonlit Blue. With Barbara Hall, Elliot's mother and co-director by his side, and with his wife Louise watching tensely in the wings, the crowds surged in a human tide towards Elliot Hall and the Moorcroft Enamels stand as soon as the doors to Hall 1 opened.

Five minutes later, the twenty-five year old managing director was writing his first order for Moorcroft Enamels. From an American store, it was worth £53,000 – more than twice the total level of orders the company, under its former name of Kingsley Enamels, had taken during the entire trade show the previous year. By the time the International Spring Fair closed, orders on Elliot's books exceeded even the total taken by Moorcroft in its Centenary Year. Elliot Kingsley Hall had arrived, and it only remained to consider how best to launch his new enamel art and have a party at the same time. Alan Wright spoke with Barbara King at Liberty about a launch, while Hugh made contact with the political machine powering a strong Labour Government to see what could be done about the party.

Two weeks later, Alan and Hugh compared notes. Liberty had agreed to stock Moorcroft Enamels – the first time the famous Regent Street store had ever carried decorated enamels in its 124 year history. Hugh had no means of verifying the fact when Liberty told him this, but the implications were pleasant. It was also easy to agree the Liberty request for an exclusive enamel limited edition. Out of Moorcroft's design archives came Narcisssus, an original William Moorcroft pottery design drawn exclusively for Liberty, probably around 1908, and put into production shortly afterwards. To fulfil his part of the bargain, Hugh had enjoyed a pleasant lunch in London with Mary Goudie, known to the world as Baroness Goudie of Roundwood. Their meeting turned out to be the precursor to an invitation for a party at the House of Lords to celebrate the arrival of Moorcroft Enamels.

Journalists who had done so much to tell the story of Moorcroft's sorties into new areas of the applied arts would all be invited, as would every member of the Design Studio. Key players in the Moorcroft Enamels workforce would also receive an invitation, along with some of the company's leading retail partners, without whose support Moorcroft Pottery itself might have drifted into oblivion twelve years earlier. For the guests, the party was an enjoyable experience, with the host Peers both courteous and helpful. One delighted American retailer was given a personalised tour of the House by a 'real live Peer'. Hugh found himself making a modest speech with no less a personage than the Lord Chancellor standing a few feet away. Even for an experienced lawyer, public speaking in the presence of the head of the legal profession is always a strain!

Just one week after the House of Lord's party, the commercial launch of Moorcroft Enamels was held at Liberty. Designer Philip Gibson represented the Design Studio; Elliot Hall attended for Moorcroft Enamels, while Mr John was on hand to answer collectors' queries about his father's design work. The Liberty launch of Moorcroft's newest business was an event to remember. Collectors came to examine the sparkling enamels, and Liberty staff were kept busy on the tills. It was one of those occasions where to have been there was something memorable. To have missed the occasion would become a cause for regret.

Of equal significance for the year 2000, Alan reminded Hugh, was Liberty's own 125th birthday party, delightfully timed to coincide with Moorcroft's millennium celebrations and the launch of Hugh's new book, *Winds of Change*. Barbara King's request for a special Moorcroft pottery limited edition piece for the occasion was greeted with broad smiles. These faded somewhat when it became known that Liberty intended to issue a design specification for all contributors to its 125th birthday. First to be consulted would be senior designer Rachel Bishop, whose task it would be to work out the implications of Liberty's requirements.

Two weeks later, the Moorcroft designer was searching through Liberty's magnificent design records, with a very serious archivist watching her every move. Inevitably Rachel felt a small twinge of regret when she found herself on the adaptation trail once again. It was the same twinge of regret she had felt adapting the work of Charles Rennie Mackintosh and William Morris several years earlier. Rachel had the international standing necessary to work on her own initiative and inspiration without involving herself in research of the work of dead men and women. She had earned the right to feel that way about her art. Rachel's reputation is that of an outstandingly original ceramic designer in her own right – a designer who, like Clarice Cliff before her, had recently been asked by Staffordshire University for permission to use her name on a new hall of residence. Despite her international reputation, Rachel still remains a true professional, and carried on with the Liberty research as the Regent Street store had asked.

*Cymric Dream.*
*Height 20 cm (8").*

Sometimes in this world the tide of events turns for the better. In Rachel's case, the tide turned because Liberty chief executive, Michele Jobling, issued a directive that Liberty 125 designs had to be "luxurious, colourful and textured". Inspired by the words, the designer felt that she had been given an inch, and promptly took a yard. The result was Cymric Dream, a superb design encompassing several features of Liberty innovation over the past century and a quarter. Some small part might have been recognised by Rex Silver, another by Archibald Knox. Threads of textured fabric pattern were all present, the whole embraced by a luxurious burst of vibrant colour. Right down to the smallest detail, there was a symmetry and style which spelt 'Liberty'. Moorcroft could not have delivered anything better. Cymric Dream was the work of an inspired designer.

At a special meeting in December 1999, held on the same day that Hugh and Maureen's daughter, Karen, gave birth to their first grandchild, Liberty approved Cymric Dream for inclusion in its birthday celebrations on 18 May 2000. The news on its own provoked a small flutter of embarrassment. The design had not yet passed through Moorcroft's own design approval process. Hugh would cope. He always had in the past. Most important of all, he recognised just how special the design was, and at a meeting with Rachel shortly afterwards he told her so.

Moorcroft was almost ready to greet the new millennium, and the Liberty 125 birthday celebrations were part of it. There was one more task to perform. As far as Hugh was concerned, the time had come to clear the Moorcroft decks of old designs, consigning them to the previous century. There they would become part of Moorcroft's colourful and honourable history. Designs carried forward into the new millennium would come solely from Rachel and her team in the Design Studio. With hindsight, the work undertaken between 1997 and 2000 would be seen as transitional. The year 2000 would witness a new dawn: the arrival of new, young designers with new ideas of their own; as such it would constitute a new chapter in the life of the world's best-loved art pottery. In this Moorcroft was fortunate. Rachel was now leading by example; her experience in the creation of design in the Moorcroft idiom was invaluable. Without her, the passage through those transitional years would have been much harder to navigate. Rachel was not a traditionalist, but an innovator. In design terms, the role she had created for herself at Moorcroft was that of a bridge between the end of an old design era and the beginning of a new one.

Moorcroft designers are asked for details of their current ideas on design. There is nothing particularly regular about the requests, which are more spontaneous than organised. Anji Davenport's particular response to a request made in early Spring was a design totally different from anything ever produced by Moorcroft in its 100 year history. Against a bleak winter landscape covered with fine snow, a fox could be seen slinking across white fields. Everyone at the Works loved the design. As if powered by its own momentum, new shapes popped up here, there and everywhere throughout the late spring and summer. With each new piece, Hugh's embarrassment increased. Ground rules in design dictated that trials should be approved at a design meeting made up of relevant directors and the senior designer. At the rate Anji's snow scene pieces were emerging from the glost kiln, a complete range would be ready before formal design approval had even been requested, let alone granted!

Hugh need not have worried. Those involved in the process of approval had already seen the design and were not in the mood to do anything other than offer favourable comment and encouragement. Those who subscribe to corporate rules and praise corporate man would find this apparently haphazard approach to the creative process totally unacceptable. Moorcroft is different, which is part of its charm. Anji's foxes were seen and praised by those involved in making them, approving them, promoting them, selling them and enjoying them. That the design might be rejected at a design meeting was something no one even considered.

In stark contrast Hugh had received from a member of the public a letter praising Moorcroft's attitude to its workforce and the esteem in which each member was held. The author of the letter turned out to be a leading modeller in the ceramic industry who specialised in figurines. The letter had been written the day after the modeller had been summoned to a 'design' meeting in her own company to discuss a 'new project'. Present were the managing director who said little, the art director who said nothing, and the sales director who spoke most of the time.

The modeller was told by the sales director that the company required a 10-inch figurine with auburn hair, wearing a yellow dress, green scarf, handbag and shoes. Most important of all, the piece had to retail at £199 – no more, no less. In the Potteries, an impetuous word to traditional directors can result in outright dismissal, often accompanied by a few patronising remarks about high interest rates, collapsing export sales due to the strength of the pound – all brought about by the Labour Government. The modeller was wise enough to keep quiet and create the figurine as the sales director had instructed. To help come to terms with a sense of genuine outrage, she decided to write to the Moorcroft Chairman instead. Hugh invited her round for a cup of tea and a talk. As he listened to the story, he was just vaguely reminded of Liberty's first thoughts on their 125 vase, and the stark contrast of the second instruction to design something luxurious, colourful and textured. At Moorcroft it was all so different. Designers are largely given a free hand. The Design Studio's first house rule is that if another company has done or has not done something, Moorcroft never knowingly follows suit. In the applied arts, Moorcroft has to remain a leader and not a copyist or follower.

Occasionally it is necessary for a designer to spend time away from the

FACING: *Woodside Farm range. Tallest vase (top left) 25 cm (10″).*

Works. Inspirational ideas are often gathered from external influences, and if Hugh attempted to assert otherwise, the designers would say that corporate man was rearing his head. At the end of the day, designers either produce new designs or they do not. Absence from the Works had to be matched by delivery. Most millennium design work needed to be completed by early May. There would inevitably be on-going work to finish particular ranges and a few special pieces required for Open Weekend at the end of May. Collectors' Christmas Weekend in November was also on the horizon. At least that was how it seemed as Spring 1999 turned gently into early summer, but appearances were deceptive.

First 1999 Open Weekend 'specials' from the Design Studio had started to appear a month or so earlier. Phil had already put forward a busy Gentian design framed with strong iris flower heads in a mix of mauve and purple as a possible

*Gentian trials. Tallest vase 25 cm (10").*

Liberty 125 design. The Gentian itself was an eye-catching blue and the colour mix carried with it a strong hint of Liberty purple. Two days later the piece was joined by a smaller vase carrying the same design, but on the 122/7 shape. Sensing a repeat of Anji's Fox design story, Hugh asked Phil to pause for a moment and consider a piece for Open Weekend instead. The designer had already done so, and produced from a cardboard box another design drawn on the statutory 'green' clay pot. The piece was called Monkshood. Designed to Moorcroft's well known 364/8 shape, Monkshood had all the characteristics of a classic, as they say. Gracious pink, yellow and cream flower heads curled their way to the top of the vase through moss-green leaves which turned into a delicate brown towards the tip.

While Hugh was thinking how much he liked Monkshood and its cream ground which faded to blue at the base, Phil produced from his artist's case four wild herb drawings, all coloured. The Moorcroft chairman found himself staring at Comfrey, Chicory, Burdock and Borage. As if that were not enough, with a final theatrical flourish Phil produced rough drawings for two more herb designs, Mallow and Tansy. All were brilliant, causing Hugh's collector's tummy to turn several violent somersaults. However, the stark reality was an absence of sufficient time for the new designs to be trialled before Open Weekend. Hugh's tummy abruptly stopped

FACING: *Collectors 1999 Open Weekend pieces. Tallest vase 25 cm (10").*

Colorado

Cape
Gooseberry

Oxalis

Aster

White Holly

Protea

Milos

Lavenham

Monkshood

Lavenham

churning and the excitement faded away. A decision on Phil's herb series was one which could wait. What Hugh was not aware of was that a well-known artistic phenomenon was about to break out in the Design Studio. Some of the designers were 'on a roll'.

To keep Monkshood company over Open Weekend, Anji Davenport had drawn Cape Gooseberry on the 98/8 shape. This fresh effort on Anji's part caused considerable relief throughout the Works, who had feared that her Woodside Farm (as Fox had become known) range might be reduced to a single piece and sacrificed on the altar of Open Weekend expediency by the Moorcroft Board. Even Emma and Nicki both found design time to bring forward a design each.

From Nicki came White Holly on a 32/5 while Emma, still in Protea mode, produced another glorious Protea flower on the increasingly popular 198/5 shape. Shirley Hayes, a designer still to achieve her full potential, had worked quietly on the 80/6 with a Palmata design involving deep red flowers with rich green leaves, all set against a dark woodsmoke ground which faded from almost black at the base of the vase to a light washed grey at the centre. Again Hugh was uncertain what to do with Palmata. His eventual conclusion was to place it with Phil's Herb series and the Gentian vases, and wait for the next design meeting. In the meantime, Shirley's alternative Oxalis design was passed for production at Open Weekend in several different colourways. Like Palmata, it was a busy design, and it would be for collectors to judge whether the piece was successful. Palmata could be simplified. Oxalis could not.

Whichever way he looked at the May 'specials', Hugh's personal favourite was Monkshood, followed closely by an unusual design created by the ever-active Debbie Hancock. Debbie is a highly skilled and efficient decorator as well as designer, who understands as well as anyone whether a design will match a given shape and which ceramic colours blend well together. Even more importantly, Debbie knows what makes a piece easy or difficult to decorate. Her personal contribution for Open Weekend was a landscape of sand-coloured mountains with trumpet-shaped white flowers in the foreground. The design perspective was simple, yet those who saw it pointed out that the piece carried a high perceived value. Desert Song Hugh called it. Colorado was the name given to it by everyone else. Hugh was asked by an American woman to tell his colleagues that Colorado was an inappropriate name. There are no deserts in Colorado, yet the design featured a desert. Desert Song was the most accurate name, but Colorado it remained. Some problems seem insoluable, even for Moorcroft! In complete contrast to Debbie's spartan landscape, Rachel's soft Milos design, intricately drawn on the 120/9 shape, had a warmth which instantly commanded attention, and a subtlety which made a purchase almost compulsive. Few were left on the shop shelves by the time the last collector set off for home.

It was always seen as a token of peace when Rachel carried a mug of tea up to Hugh's room at the Works. It is also a sign that she has something important to say. On the day in question, the tea arrived in the Chairman's favourite barrel mug decorated with Rachel's butterflies. In sign language, that also meant she had a favour to ask. It was, the senior designer intoned slowly, time for Moorcroft to consider stained glass design techniques. If book illustrators could use them, why not ceramic designers?

Unusually for him, Hugh sat back and listened. Rachel's idea for her special millennium contribution was a three-panelled design showing the Archangel Gabriel, the Garden of Eden and a scene from the Great Flood. There would be no Adam and Eve – just a tree with a snake wound round the trunk. The boats would be tossed on stormy seas, and at the top of each piece there would be a white dove. As an idea it was different, and Hugh was always comfortable with Rachel's ever-changing approach to design. The sailing boat panel would be coloured in shades of blue, brown and cream. Because Hugh said nothing at all, Rachel took the silence as a signal to move forward with the project. It was Hugh's sudden suggestion that her earlier 'coloured beads' design was too good to be wasted on a limited edition and should be converted into a full range that made the senior designer's smile vanish. 'Don't chance your luck', she said and left the room.

If Rachel, Phil and Debbie were 'on a roll', it seemed that Jeanne McDougall lacked the inspiration capable of conversion into a piece for Open Weekend. Subtle hints failed to stir her, although the designer told everyone that she was 'working at home'. Less than three weeks before Open Weekend, Jeanne brought forward Lavenham which was hurried through the design approval process. Drawn on the 120/9 vase and a 15cm coaster, Lavenham made a strong impact. Purple was the theme colour, and there was absolutely no doubt about the identity of Lavenham's creator. The piece was in Jeanne's unique style. Collectors loved it, and Lavenham sold out totally over the three days it was available. Seventeen vases and thirty-five coasters were made. 'No time to make any more,' was all the production director could bring himself to say.

# SEVENTEEN

# Emergency Stops and Experimental Starts

Less than twenty-four hours after the close of the 1999 Open Weekend, the Edwards found themselves on holiday deep in the heart of France's Massif Central. Although it was almost summer, a forest of wild flowers still nodded their colourful heads along the roadside. Poppies, cornflowers and ox-eye daisies made a brilliant display of red, white and blue, while meadow after meadow of ragged robin turned each field into the colours of a summer sunset. A casual observer might have been tempted to conclude that Maureen wanted to stop and look at them all. Hugh had long since learned how to drive with his wife in the passenger seat. Occasionally others found her habits as a passenger difficult, and at times even disturbing. If there were flowers or sheep about, she would often shout 'stop', causing her husband to slam on the brakes in what he hoped would be a perfect emergency stop. Thirty-four years earlier, his driving examiner must have known that one day this particular technique would become important to the Moorcroft Chairman, and failed him twice on driving tests for failing to stop quickly enough.

Soon after the Edwards' arrival in France, Hugh was called upon several times to stop without warning. On one occasion, after waving apologetically to the complaining driver of a Citroen van travelling hard on his car's tail, Hugh was treated to a sight the like of which he had never seen before. Thousands upon thousands of wild white narcissi covered the hillsides as far as the eye could see. When gusts of warm wind blew from the Cevennes to the south, the flowers moved in waves of white colour as if wishing to bend to the power and majesty of the mountains, forests and streams still gushing noisily as the remaining winter snows melted into summer. Perhaps William Moorcroft had seen a similar sight back in 1908 when his Narcissus design for Liberty had first been conceived. The enamel vase made specially for the launch of Moorcroft Enamels at Liberty had proved to be a runaway success, but by the millennium it would be part of Moor-

FACING: *Fruit Garden. Tallest vase 17cm (7").*

croft's history. New designs would quickly take its place in the same way that Anemone Blue, Magnolia Ivory, Violet, Bramble and Poppy, Sweet Briar and the New Forest series would all be replaced with something new — perhaps better, but certainly exciting and fresh.

At a design meeting held on the 17 May, many of the new designs brought forward for approval had been rated highly and moved on for final trials. Others were quietly referred back to their designers for revision. To the everlasting joy of everyone at the Works, Anji's Woodside Farm was finally approved on no fewer than ten pieces to form a novel and unusually coloured range. It was a curious experience for all those involved in the design approval process. Had Woodside Farm been rejected, there was a strongly held view that the decorating shop would have 'downed brushes' and walked out. Anji christened the range 'Woodside' Farm after her childhood home. Everyone about the Works agreed with this choice.

It was also an open secret that Nicola Slaney's Fruit Garden had translated into a lovely range of twelve pieces, each one of which had a number of jubilant supporters in the Nile Street decorating shop. Pre-eminent among these was Sue Fairhead, the famous Moorcroft decorator who had recently returned to the company after an absence of more than ten years. During her time away, Sue had not only brought up two children to school age, but had also successfully fought off cancer. Her principal role at Moorcroft was to train many of the art pottery's aspiring young decorators, and support and praise for a new design coming from someone

FACING: *Fruit Garden. Height of jug 24 cm (9½").*

*Sue Fairhead (top left) with Joanne Walton and sample training coasters (below).*

whose name is spoken of in the same breath as the legendary Wendy Mason was a real compliment. Sue's speciality had been the painting of fruit, and it was likely that many of her pupils would decorate Nicola's Fruit Garden range.

Training was scheduled to feature strongly on the Moorcroft agenda well after the year 2000. Rachel's original training designs were due for a change. Most were becoming more difficult to sell in the Moorcroft factory shop, a sure sign in an art pottery that change was necessary. In the applied arts, everything tends to fade in collectability with the passage of time. Sometimes fashion dictates a change of mood; sometimes colours become too difficult to mix with the degree of accuracy required. Reasons are legion. It had taken more than sixty years for Anemone Blue to fade into oblivion. In sharp contrast, other designs had remained popular for only very short periods indeed.

Rachel had already taken up the design cause of Cobridge Stoneware and was currently working on four design themes all at the same time. This was not the right moment to divert her energy into designs for new training pieces. As a result, Debbie Hancock, decorator and designer, was asked to come forward with something new for Moorcroft's trainees to work on. The request for a new range of training pieces was made to Debbie halfway through April, and by Open Weekend at the end of May, Cherries, Apples, Quince, Grapes and a simple Rhododendron design were all ready for Moorcroft collectors. Cherries were instantly popular, but Quince and Apple fought together in the same colour zone, a sure sign that one or the other of them would be a very early candidate for replacement. In the event, it was Quince that was quietly withdrawn three months later, and in its place came Debbie's re-statement of Moorcroft's ever-popular Plum theme. To produce trainee designs in just four shapes for each design proved a wise move for collectors and trainee decorators alike. What the collector of training pieces would not have known was that each shape had been carefully selected to tax the trainee to the full. So too had the designs themselves. As soon as a trainee had mastered the design on one complete set of shapes, he or she would be transferred to another more difficult design. In that way decorating and tube-lining skills move forward in a planned way, while collectors have something new to admire.

After Moorcroft's new Phoenix Works in Nile Street had been opened by Government Minister Richard Caborn MP, Keith Dawson moved the bulk of the company's lamp production to the new works. Hugh had talked about poles and pyramids for some years now, and his colleagues had come to think in similar

FACING: *Sample training pieces. Tallest vase 18cm. (7").*

Trout tiles

terms. The transfer of the lamp business to the Phoenix Works was logical. Lamps were already a significant and fast-growing part of Moorcroft's business. In the world of retail, lamps are seen primarily as furniture, not as collectables. They are not part of the same market, evidenced by the fact that when the furniture market goes flat, the collectables market can still remain very much alive or vice-versa. To increase lamp production as Keith proposed was yet another way to secure Moorcroft's long-term future. Because the two retail market places were independent of each other, lamps added another brick of long-term security to the base of the Moorcroft pyramid.

But Keith had more than just lamps in mind. Ever since he had joined Moorcroft from Pilkington Tiles, the production director had nurtured plans to start making Moorcroft tiles, although in a modest way at the outset. Both 15cm and 20cm tiles had already been modelled, blocked and cased in readiness for the designers. The Design Studio, however, was too busy with other work to involve themselves in decorated tiles which were not officially on their agenda. Admittedly Rachel had drawn a one-off Sweet Briar tile, while Phil Gibson had produced single, double and treble designs in both Trout and Flame of the Forest. After studying De Morgan tile designs, Shirley Hayes brought forward a series of Bird of Paradise designs on single tiles, while Anji introduced Woodside Farm as both a single and a double. Not to be out-manoeuvred, Jeanne McDougall stunned everyone with her upright three-tile tableaux California. Later still, Phil came back with a two-tile Flamingo de-

Puffin tiles

sign to complement work he was undertaking on Everglade Flamingos for the millennium catalogue. And so it was. Moorcroft suddenly had tiles!

The question was what to do with them all. Keith wanted to make tiles, but by the time he was ready to start, the Nile Street factory was full. Before it was built, Hugh had forecast that the Phoenix Works would be operating at full capacity within four years. The reality turned out to be very different. Four months after its formal opening on the 16 September 1998, the factory was full. The Board decided that the experimental tile tableaux already made would all be sold over Open Weekend at their correct market prices to gauge collector reaction. Provided that reaction was enthusiastic, production would follow in a limited way after the arrival of the millennium. Once a second new Moorcroft factory had been built, something more serious could be considered. In practice, this meant

*Woodside Farm tiles*

that production of Keith's tiles had been approved – but only to test the water. Over the three days of Open Weekend, collectors indicated and demonstrated their approval by buying almost every tile on offer.

As the Edwards' car wound its way up and down the gorges of the Massif Central and across the high, windswept plateaux of the Cevennes, Hugh and Maureen talked together about designers and designs. Enthusiasm for Emma's Frangipani had been little more than lukewarm at the May design meeting, and the designer had been asked to reconsider both the perspective of the design itself and the use of a grey wash as the background colour to the frangipani flowers. If anyone should ever conclude that designers are weak, inadequate people

unable to come to terms with the reverses that life occasionally throws in the path of human endeavour, they would be seriously mistaken. Just as Nicola Slaney had done a year earlier when her Swamp Hen, Pink Orchid and Indian Summer designs were held back from mainstream production, Emma literally returned to the drawing board to bring forward an acceptable answer to each criticism made.

Shortly before his holiday in France, Hugh had been shown by Emma a redrawn Frangipani design with a number of colour and perspective options, all shown on different parts of the same trial piece. The designer had painted the trial herself, and the options on offer were numerous. At the base of the vase appeared a wash of light blue not dissimilar to the colour of the sea on Emma's successful Kiribati design. The blue faded into cream but not before a tiny stylised atoll had been drawn low down on the vase, out of which grew a stem topped with a vibrant cluster of frangipani flowers. This use of the stem made the design seem almost surreal. It was as if the delicate pink flowerheads had reached the sky and burst open across the whole horizon to clothe the top of the vase in colour.

Before he had time to comment, Emma produced another surprise from her bubblewrap for Hugh to look at. Everyone in the Design Studio knew there was a strong likelihood that the Moorcroft Violet range would be discontinued before the year 2000 arrived. Violet was a busy geometric design much loved by a small but vociferous section of the Moorcroft collecting public. If it disappeared, something geometric would be needed to take its place. Sales for Violet were in decline, and with or without the millennium its discontinuation was virtually inevitable. The problem was that to design in the geometric idiom required special skills. Rachel was more than able to produce a geometric design. Her 1994 Heartsease already bore a passing testimony to that. Subsequent rumblings about 'stained glass' design confirmed the view that geometric work was never far from her mind, but Rachel had other work on hand and discussion about geometric design fell silent.

What Emma produced was a superb geometric design, totally abstract, on Moorcroft's 32/5 shape. Soft, dark green fusing into purple gave the piece a simplicity which was breathtaking. The substitute for Violet had arrived. Indigo was the name bestowed upon it at a subsequent design meeting where ten delicate pieces were recommended to the Moorcroft Board for production as a range.

Hugh's instinctive reaction was to shower praise on the smiling young designer. The Frangipani perspective was almost unique in Moorcroft's art, and yet

FACING: *Indigo. Tallest vase 15 cm (6″).*

the improvement in the design somehow justified the original criticism. Designs were now ready to fill the space left by both the departing Magnolia Ivory and Violet. After agreeing the preferred Frangipani option with the designer, both it and Indigo moved forward for final trials. The designs were young, fresh and would be relatively inexpensive to produce, and the millennium catalogue would be richer for their presence.

By the time the Edwards finally reached the flowery grasslands of the Cevennes, there was total unaminity between husband and wife on two other designs. While Emma's Hellebore had failed to make the grade at the design meeting, her pretty little Hepatica almost stole the show. The subtle use of purple and cream put the design into an unusual colour zone for Moorcroft, and yet the over-

all result was as fine and simple as even the most experienced of those present had ever seen. Emma had first drawn Hepatica on the 72/6 shape, which Phil had used for his 1999 Collectors' Club vase. Keith had no problems with the use of the 72 shape for a second time. Indeed, it was Phil's Collectors' Club design itself which raised a few smiles at the meeting, coming as it did with yellow Wisteria flowers. Phil was already in the mood to speak firmly with the first 'expert' ready to point out that there was no such thing as a yellow wisteria. Everyone at Moorcroft knew that yellow wisteria did not exist, and that included Phil himself. An art pottery is not necessarily in the business of reality. If collectors want total reality, then they should turn their attention to photography or trans-

*Ashwood Hepatica.*
*Height 10 cm (4").*

fer prints produced by machines.

After everyone had had their say, Emma was asked to produce further Hepatica design work on different shapes. In so doing, those present acknowledged that Hepatica would end up as a small range, rather like Nicola's Hellebore. Nicola had introduced Hellebore to the design meeting drawn on the 92/11 shape, and for once those present had nothing to say. The design was in total harmony with the shape, and the colour was in total harmony with the design. It was already understood that horticultural accuracy of line would be something to put for comment to John Massey, the man in charge at Ashwood Nurseries, before production started. This applied to Emma's Hepatica as well. Both designers had drawn their inspiration following a visit to the remarkable Ashwood

FACING: *Ashwood Hepatica range. Tallest vase 15 cm (6").*

*Hellebores. The Ashwood Hellebore range; facing a detail form one of the pots. Height of tall vase (top left) 27cm (11").*

Nurseries, and it was only fitting that John Massey should have the last word on the subject. By now, everyone at Moorcroft hoped that the Government's special commission for the Millennium Dome would not come through and whisk the Hellebores and Hepaticas away. If nothing further was heard, both designs would be available for Moorcroft retailers world-wide – including, no doubt, Ashwood Nurseries themselves.

The Moorcroft Board went further. The Hellebore and Hepatica ranges would remain exclusive to Ashwood Nurseries until 19 February 2000. This

Ashwood Hepatica at the Royal Horticultural Society
Photograph courtesy of Photos Horticultural Picture Library

would be the date of a special Moorcroft pro-motion with Nicola and Emma in attendance. In return, John Massey would ensure that the two ranges would be displayed at the Royal Horticultural Society Show on 15 February 2000 for the world's connoisseurs of flowers to look at. After the Ashwood Nursery promo-tion, the two ranges would become available to Moorcroft's retailers world-wide.

After sixteen weeks of total devotion to her Jerusalem masterpiece, Nicola Slaney pro-duced colour trials for the massive vase on tiles, which started to emerge from the Nile Street glost kiln. Most had a distinctly Arabic flavour brought about by a clever use of light blue, aquamarine and cobalt interspersed with touches of light green. Nicola's natural colour zone is blue, and with Jerusalem she was on home territory. Next time, Hugh teased, she should enter alien territory and design something from a red colour base.

For those who give their lives to Moorcroft and its art throughout the year, Open Weekend is the high point on their calendar. It is an almost unique oppor-tunity to meet collectors and discuss with them their likes and dislikes, favourite designs and so on. For collectors, Open Weekend brings Moorcroft to life. No longer is it just a story about lovely pieces of art pottery, but about the men and women behind the pots, their ambition, dedication, love of their work and artistry.

The first of the three-day 1999 Open Weekend had been fine; the second had been wet, while the third remained overcast throughout with strong bursts of

FACING: *Open Weekend Voyager vase. Height 25 cm (10").*

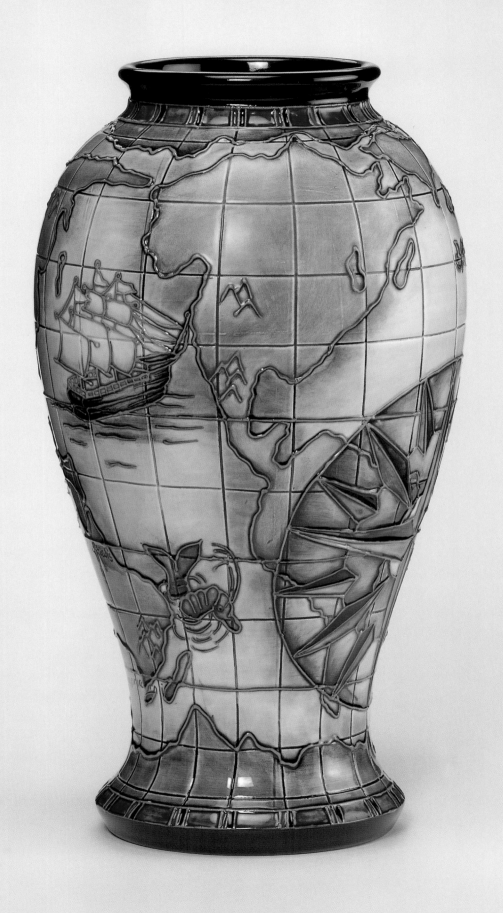

wind which rattled the tarpaulin of the marquee, occasionally causing auction-eer Peter Blood's microphone to crackle ominously. Among the staff offerings, some spectacular prices were achieved. Most prized of all was Voyager designed by Alicia Amison. Drawn on the classic 46/10 baluster shape, the design showed an old map of the world, complete with stylised compass rose coloured simply in shades of brown, green and white. For the first time ever, the average price for all nine pieces of Voyager auctioned over Open Weekend exceeded £1000, a superb achievement for a young artist/designer who a year earlier was still at art school!

Two months later, the first Voyager production trials emerged, not from the Moorcroft glost kiln, but from the Cobridge Stoneware kiln. Voyager would represent the stoneware company in the millennium. Another young designer's star was in the ascendant, except that this time it was the collectors themselves who had forced Moorcroft to acknowledge her talent.

All decorating shop designs sold well at Open Week-end, while Moorcroft's first original head and shoulders model of a young girl sold for more than £500 on each of the three days. Just as pleasing was the strength of a novel sculptured tile temporarily called Sea of Dreams. Sea of Dreams also sold for well over five hundred pounds. This was exceptionally good news for Cobridge Stoneware, as well, who were destined to offer both the model of the young girl and the sculptured tile in a new section of their own millennium catalogue.

*Marie and Mark Penkethman*

For the second year running, Marie Penkethman, one of Moorcroft's most skilled tube-liners, had designed the 1999 Open Weekend mug. The original idea had been that the design on the mug would remain both special and simple, with collectors free to ask for their own personal message to be inscribed on the base. The first such mug had been designed in 1991, with the 1997 centennial design coming from Rachel herself. With design support now available Rachel had moved on to other things, leaving Marie Penkethman to bring forward designs for the Moorcroft 1998 and 1999 Open Weekend mug. Back in 1998, Marie had designed for Collectors' Open Weekend a mug decorated with aquilegias in a pleasant mix of purple and pink. Called Floral Elegance, the piece sold well, but by the time the 1999 event closed, collectors had shown their deeper appreciation of Marie's work by ordering a record number of mugs decorated with the Italian Bell Flower. It was left to Marie's husband, Mark, to make them! Mark Penkethman had left Royal Doulton early in 1998, and Keith Dawson was quick to see his true potential. Today, Mark is Works Manager in the Nile Street factory and with both husband and wife taking a leading role in the day-to-day life of Moorcroft.

For the Design Studio members present, Open Weekend 1999 turned out to be three consecutive days of aching wrists. All were asked to sign pieces. It was Debbie Hancock who had most to complain about, however. Every one of the 250 pieces in her Samarkand Lily limited edition sold out, while her new designs for trainees, in the words of factory shop manager Michele Nixon, 'almost literally walked'. Only three months later, a Samarkand Lily sold at Christies South Kensington for £240, an increase of 37 per cent on the Open Weekend sale price!

Antiques Roadshow expert Henry Sandon gave a refreshing Open Weekend lecture to collectors on the history of tube-lining over the previous 250 years and its relevance to Moorcroft. After that he was spotted browsing intently in the factory shop before deciding to acquire an exceptionally well tube-lined and decorated Flame of the Forest lamp! There were, of course, rather fewer trials available for collectors than in the previous year. Collectors' Christmas Weekend in November had seen to that. The more important thing, Hugh confided to his wife as they looked at the distant horizons of the Auvergne, was that the collectors enjoyed themselves. Collecting, like a good holiday, should be fun.

*Open Weekend mugs. Top: 2000 – Cathedral Bells.*
*Bottom left: 1998 – Floral Elegance.*
*Bottom Right: 1999 – Italian Bell Flower.*

# EIGHTEEN

# Moorcroft Goes for Gold

Throughout the 1999 Open Weekend, Hugh found himself watching collectors as they sifted through the pots on offer to find the one which pleased them most. Everyone selected for different reasons. A man wearing a blue anorak examined seven Samarkand Lily vases before making up his mind which one to buy, while a young lady with auburn hair and a freckled face with a permanent smile settled on Emma Bossons' trial Fiji with the fawn ground fading to green, touched here and there with a faint hint of purple. That particular trial was the one Hugh had reluctantly abandoned when it came up for design approval. Now the auburn haired lady was about to take it away. The greener version of Emma's Fiji vase was already in production as part of the Dateline Series. The green version had always been the designer's favourite, and judging by sales reports from Alan Wright, Steven Swann and the rest of the Moorcroft sales team, Emma's judgement had been sound. Even so, Hugh felt a small twinge of envy as the discarded trial was wrapped in tissue and bubblewrap in readiness for its journey to a new home.

As an incorrigible collector himself, Hugh would often stand back and watch other collectors exercise freedom of choice. He had long since abandoned the idea of owning an example of every single design Moorcroft had ever made. Indeed, he had even come to terms with the idea that he would never own examples of every piece made since he became involved in the company back in 1986. Collecting is not just about accumulating quantity. Collecting is all about quality, an understanding of that strange tingle a collector sometimes feels at the tip of his or her fingers when touching a fine piece of Moorcroft for the first time. Once the fingers respond, the brain takes over.

This can be good or bad in collecting terms, depending entirely on the purpose of the acquisition. If the motive is solely investment, there is always a lurking danger that the piece will become stale, ultimately provoking dissatisfaction in its owner's mind. Once a collector leaves the reliable world of Moorcroft re-

FACING: *Jerusalem. Height 66 cm (26").*

Jerusalem. Additional panels.

tailers and enters the darker parts of the secondary market, it becomes necessary to rely on dealers – and dealers thrive on mistakes such as this. Buy in haste and repent with your dealer at leisure is what they say. It is also one of the reasons why pieces of Moorcroft occasionally return to a new life in the secondary market. But for the erstwhile owner, the secondary market experience can sometimes leave a sour taste. What is so often forgotten is that although the sale price achieved in the secondary market may turn a disposal into a profit on the original cost, the dealer has first to take a profit. Nobody should complain. The auction houses as well as dealers have to earn their living. Only after secondary market dealer or auction house profits have been taken do collectors receive the net proceeds of sale. It sometimes comes as a shock to discover that a piece which has actually increased in value still nets out to the seller at less than cost. As a result, it is crucial that a collector is up to date both on secondary market values and on current retail prices, and is aware that dealers and auction houses need profit margins in order to survive.

The pure joy of collecting either new Moorcroft or old is the first reaction of the tummy, and whether it does a somersault of joy on seeing a new piece for the first time. If it does, and the collector is afterwards lucky enough to feel the tingle of quality through sensitive finger tips, the purchase will always be satisfying. If it turns into a good investment in the long run, so much the better. A good collector knows which piece to buy; because of this a collection of real quality pieces is more likely, which then with luck can be sold profitably at a later date.

Eventually, the man with the blue anorak decided which Samarkand Lily to buy. Initially the man's tummy would have told him that he had made the right choice on design, but after that, like all really good collectors, he set about using his fingers, his eyes and his brain to identify the piece which he personally believed to be the best out of the many pieces of Samarkand Lily on offer. The collector knew just how lucky he was. He had the freedom to exercise personal choice. Fifty years on, there would be only a single Samarkand Lily on the dealer's stall or carrying an auctioneer's tag at an auction house. The original price paid would almost certainly be irrelevant. Value depends mostly upon overall quality of design, shape and condition. Age and rarity add a dimension of their own.

Those involved in making Moorcroft's Lamia range know that the most difficult colour effect to achieve is the yellow pigment forming part of the ground colour. Some pieces emerge from the kiln with a whiteish cream finish while others carry subtle overtones of yellow with varying intensity of colour. For Hugh, the rich yellow pieces are the most prized, in much the same way as pieces of Hazledene made in the early years of the twentieth century, and carrying Moorcroft's rare yellow glaze, are among some of the most sought after in the salerooms.

Elise Adams recalls once watching a collector take two and a half hours to decide on the best piece of 'almost perfect' Lamia to take home from the Moorcroft factory shop out of the forty or more pieces on offer in varying shapes and sizes. When the Collectors' Club Secretary asked why that particular piece had been selected, the answer was simple and to the point: "The yellow. I like the yellow." For Hugh, that story went to the heart of collecting. It was an exercise of choice, not a choice between different designs but a living choice among a number of pieces carrying the same design with many slight variations in colour. Fortunately for Moorcroft, people have different tastes and tend to like different shapes, different colours, different designs and different sizes. Everyone reacts to Moorcroft differently, in the same way that every piece of Moorcroft is inevitably different. That is all part of its individuality.

By the time the Edwards returned from their holiday in the Massif Central, Nicola's Jerusalem vase had started to develop in terms of colour. On 12 September, six months after she started to work on the project, the first full trial emerged from Moorcroft's glost kiln in all its glory. The piece was huge, certainly the largest single vase Moorcroft had ever made. Colours paid homage to the Islamic traditions of the Middle East as well as the most holy city on earth. From one perspective there was the Western (Wailing) Wall; from another the Church of the Holy Sepulchre; while from the third the Dome of the Rock could be seen in all its shimmering glory. Only fifty pieces would be made, and the price would be as large as the piece itself. Nobody criticised or complained. Jerusalem represented half a year of Nicola Slaney's life, and in committing herself to the work, she was placed firmly among the great ceramic designers of her time. Hugh was proud of her, and said so.

Late spring and early summer were busy times for Emma Bossons. With her revised Frangipani design moving on with full design approval behind it, the range settled down to a manageable thirteen pieces plus eight lamps. Its predecessor, Magnolia Ivory, had first been introduced in 1976, and its demise in 1999 was not unexpected among those collectors who saw Moorcroft's art as a story evolving year by year, decade by decade. The moment design stands still, the suc-

FACING: Top left: Frangipani Flowers. FACING AND ABOVE: Frangipani range. Tallest vase 25 cm (10").

cess of an art pottery will move into reverse. The process of design is restless. Just as significantly, not everyone in this world is a millionaire. Always inexpensive, Magnolia Ivory had survived for 23 years; it was now time to let it slide away into the secondary market and the tender, loving embrace of the dealers and auction houses. Anemone Blue was also about to become part of the heritage of the previous century. Eventually, as for all things no longer in production, the dealers, auction houses and buyers will be the ones to assess the true value of a treasured piece of Magnolia Ivory or Anemone Blue.

The price paid for any piece of Moorcroft in the secondary market is of no benefit to Moorcroft itself. It is a competitor sale, just like the sale of a piece of Royal Doulton or Wedgwood. A purchaser of contemporary Moorcroft helps keep the company alive. At the same time he or she will have the chance to learn about the creative process which turned Emma's Hepatica from a flash of pure inspiration into a living design involving a soft, rich mix of cream and purple. Emma drew just seven small pieces and a tile for the range. Hepatica, like all good designs, was simple. Frangipani was the same, and so too was Nicola Slaney's gentle and warm lily design, once a year plate called 'Tiger Lily' and now called Anna. Between them, all three designs would fill the space created by the departure of Magnolia Ivory and Anemone Blue. The new designs would be available for Moorcroft collectors at modest prices, which would encourage new collectors and provide something different, new and exciting for existing collectors world-wide.

*Wisteria. Height 15 cm (6").*

Phil Gibson's yellow Wisteria was launched to an enthusiastic public in August 1999. By that time, Elise Adams had developed a small neurosis about the flower itself. She, more than anyone, continued to worry that collectors would complain there was no such thing as a yellow wisteria. Eventually even Elise came to believe collectors would accept it, in the same way they had accepted blue roses. In 1993 Moorcroft had produced a small number of blue rose pieces quite successfully, and no one had ever complained about the colour. It was unlikely that yellow Wisteria would be any different. Moorcroft is not about realism, but about stories, myths and dreams, about black tulips just as much as red tulips, red roses and blue roses. The first to order Phil's yellow Wisteria vase as a collector was John Massey of Ashwood Nurseries himself. As one of the

FACING: *Anna. Tallest vase 25 cm (10").*

world's leading horticulturalists, his purchase spoke volumes. Elise now had a ready-made answer for anyone who queried Moorcroft's mythical yellow Wisteria.

Whichever hat Hugh found himself wearing, Moorcroft combined both pain and pleasure. It was with great pleasure that he heard the yellow Wisteria vase had sold more pieces in its first month than any of its predecessors in the Collectors' Club series. That satisfied his instincts both as a collector and as a businessman. Less pleasurable was a recollection dating back a year when Hugh found himself nominated as Businessman of the Year in a competition organised by the British Business Awards Association. He had come second, and as the saying goes there are no prizes for coming second.

His nomination the following year by a collector who should have known better saw Hugh once again down to the final three. This time, however, he carried the winner's statuette in silver and gold back to the Works. Quite separately, Cobridge Stoneware were runners up in the Innovation of the Year Award. Hugh was probably more pleased at the Cobridge success, but as a man without any expectations about life, he was genuinely surprised the following day when the Nile Street decorating shop broke into spontaneous applause when he entered the room. Life has a habit of twisting and turning, and in the applied arts reaction to success never follows a set pattern of rules. Some people love you for it. Others hate you.

Collecting in general does not follow a set pattern either. It is a mix of the thrill of discovery coupled with an unfailing ability to distinguish the good from the bad and indifferent. Jerusalem was not just good. It was a great piece of ceramic art, but one which would be enjoyed by relatively few people. Because of the price and the small number of the edition, this was inevitable. Moving in parallel to Jerusalem, however, were three designs from three different designers, all of which eased their way into the millennium catalogue as limited editions at much lower prices.

Everyone who saw it at Open Weekend had rated Beverley Wilkes' Meknes at Night as effective as her original Meknes design. All pieces on offer were quickly snapped up despite a price tag of just under £900. The trouble (or the blessing, depending on your point of view) is that Beverley Wilkes produces only one new design a year, or rarely two. Invariably her designs are good, well thought through, spontaneous and original. At the May design meeting she offered her Elephants vase drawn to the 8/6 shape. Although Hugh was not entirely sure

FACING: *Meknes at Night (above): Height* 22cm (9"). 
*Kerala (below): Height* 15cm (6").

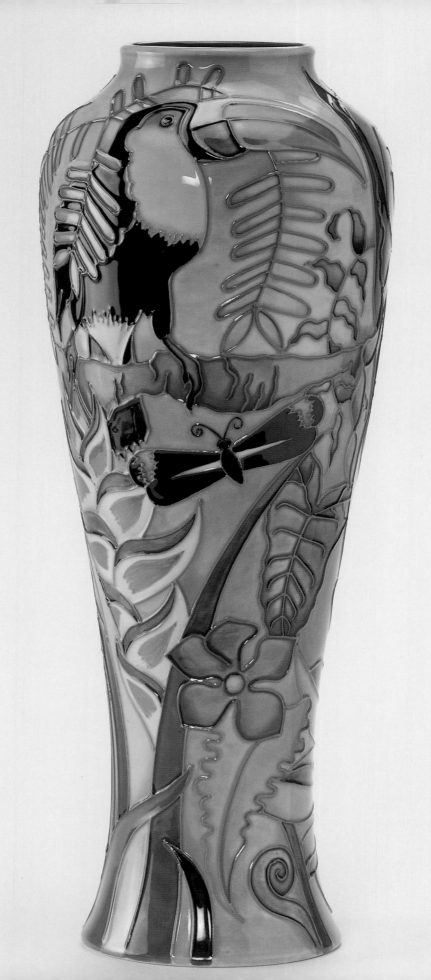

about the piece himself, everyone else present swamped it with praise. Shortly afterwards, a decision was made that Beverley's Elephants would be available for the millennium in a limited edition of 400 pieces. Elise Adams called it Kerala after the southern tropical state in India. The forests of Kerala are the natural habitat of Asian elephants, and no festival or celebration is complete without an elephant procession, just like the procession on Beverley's Kerala vase. While everyone was praising Kerala, Hugh whispered in Beverley's ear about a possible adaptation of her Meknes design for the year 2000. The designer smiled, but said nothing. For the moment, that was good enough for Hugh.

These days, Hugh is the first to admit the impossibility for those involved in the creative process of design to get it right first time. This extends to those charged with the responsibility of approving designs. Back in the early days with Dark Lady, Jeanne McDougall, Hugh had been wrong. Fortunately for Moorcroft his colleagues had been right, and Martinique had wafted into the Moorcroft catalogue like a breath of fresh air. The wheel had turned full circle by the time of the May design meeting. Jeanne was in hospital having her tonsils removed, and it was left to Hugh to speak for her new design on his own.

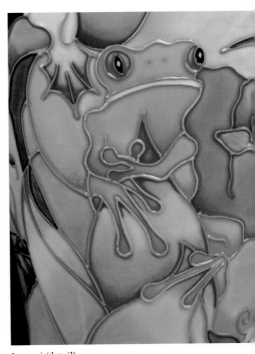

*Jaraqui (detail)*

With the success of Arizona, California and Florida following hard on the heels of Martinique itself, Jeanne's latest offering was in no danger of an unfavourable reception in her absence. After a moment of silence everyone spoke at once. Mr John reminded everyone that his wife adored frogs, but the frog was a minor feature. Standing before the meeting, perched perfectly on the 121/14 shape, was the most mischievous toucan imaginable. To pre-empt premature comment, Hugh advised the meeting that there were one or two changes the designer herself wished to make. Words were superfluous. Toucan was unquestionably ready to fly into the millennium catalogue as a limited edition of 250. An elated but still sick Jeanne was told of the decision shortly afterwards. Scarcely able to speak she agreed that the vase should be called Jaraqui, the natural home of toucans in their Amazon rainforest habitat. Everyone agreed.

Rachel Bishop, who attends design meetings as senior designer, saw her

FACING: *Jaraqui. Height 35cm (14″).*

ABOVE AND FACING: *Gypsy. Diameter of charger* 35cm (14″).

own new design (later called Gypsy) approved for production. Originally brought forward for design approval on the 92/11 shape, the final trial was a 10-inch version of the 304 shape, previously used by Emma Bossons for her larger 304/15 King Protea. Hugh had no doubts about the piece at all and seriously regretted that it had not already been transformed into a range rather than brought forward as a possible limited edition. It was vintage Rachel Bishop with a haunting feel of the past already encapsulated in his own favourite Ryden Lane design. This new offering was a rich combination of pink, purple and blue and it felt good to touch. Hugh's tummy had long since turned its tell-tale somersaults, while Mr John, who had first described the design as 'coloured beads', climbed down from his original diagnosis and offered support.

Not surprisingly, those present approved the design for production. Hugh scarcely heard the verdict. Even as he stared at the vase, it seemed to grow in quality. The rich swirling purple leaves swept gracefully up the body of the vase before exploding into a myriad of small coloured petals shaped like a fan at the top. This vase, with its cool blue ground and just a subtle hint of mauve and pink, was nothing like a collection of coloured beads. It had the quality of greatness last seen in Rachel's famous Love in a Mist and Lamia designs. Put simply, it would be difficult for collectors not to fall in love with it. A full range was something to be fought for at the next Board meeting. It was something he had to raise once more with the designer, who had helped him so much in the lead up to Moorcroft's centenary. As a limited edition it would be wasted. If Gypsy was to become a range, the more immediate problem was to identify another limited edition to take its place.

FACING AND ABOVE: *Gypsy. Tallest vase 27 cm (11").*

# NINETEEN

# On the Brink

For Keith Dawson a pub was a familiar place in his childhood years, the heart of a community of real people and the place where miners, stokers and placers came each day to quench their thirst after a real day's work. Keith should know. He was born in the Miners Arms at Brown Edge, Stoke on Trent, where his father was licence holder for twenty years, and where his mother worked day after day running the business. Throughout his life, his father suffered long and arduous shifts underground in the sludge, dust and grit of the coal face before coming home to help his wife behind the bar. Forty-five years of working in the Chatterley Whitfield mine took its savage and inevitable toll on his health in later years, and Keith's father finally died of pneumonia precipitated by pneumoconiosis.

When Hugh agreed terms to buy the Dog and Partridge pub on the corner of Hot Lane and Nile Street immediately opposite the Cobridge Stoneware Works, it was, for Keith, rather like the prospect of returning home. An attractive Grade II listed building of similar vintage to the Moorcroft factory in Sandbach Road, the Dog and Partridge was the last remaining piece in Moorcroft's property jigsaw puzzle to slot into place before final plans for a second Nile Street factory could be made. It had taken Moorcroft more than a year to close negotiations to buy the Dog and Partridge, but even before the contract had been signed Keith confided in his colleagues that one of his outstanding ambitions was to have an office in a pub. His father would have approved. It seemed that in the fullness of time, Keith would have every chance of achieving this particular ambition. The new Macintyre works in Nile Street site would house a modern millennium factory to cope with Moorcroft's ever-increasing lamp business, its revitalised export drive, and Keith's own beloved tile project.

Over Open Weekend, all the tile tableaux had sold well at prices which reflected the true cost of making them. Keith had discovered that Rachel's 21 cm Sweet Briar tile had the same amount of artwork on it as a 7/7 vase – much more

FACING: *Cathedral. Height 40cm (16").*

*Rock of Ages. Tallest vase
35 cm (14").*

than a casual comparison would suggest. It was the same for all tiles, of course, but the cost implications had to be born in mind. Tiles would be made at the Macintyre works creating up to 180 new jobs over six years. Moorcroft plans also included an ambitious second phase in Nile Street comprising a new crèche for 42 babies, and a much-needed Visitor Centre.

Later still there were plans for a second factory, this time on the Nile Street frontage, perhaps to house Okra's glass business or Elliot Hall's burgeoning enamels operation. Plans might change; a totally new company might join the Moorcroft family group. The only certain facts were that Cobridge Stoneware needed to expand its business as quickly as possible and take over the Phoenix Works in their entirety. It was left to Keith Dawson to assess the Dog and Partridge as a possible training school for Moorcroft, albeit a temporary one. That was the first goal to be achieved. For a man whose other ambitions included a desire to climb Mont Blanc alone, Keith Dawson's application for planning permission to change the permitted use of the Dog and Partridge was a relatively simple manoeuvre.

By the end of May, it was clear to everyone that although Keith's production increases for Moorcroft were moving according to plan, they were not moving ahead of plan. As a result there was insufficient extra production to fuel Emma Bossons' and Nicola Slaney's projected visit to meet Australian and New Zealand collectors in September. Hugh's first task on his return from holiday in June was to tell the two Moorcroft ambassadors that their visit would have to be postponed until March in the year 2000. Put simply, there was little to be gained from stirring Antipodean interest in Moorcroft if the pots themselves would take months to arrive. Moorcroft's distributor, Philip Allen, would need a good stock on hand for collectors, and it was Moorcroft's task to ensure he had the required stock more or less on call to support the visit. The millennium celebrations in the United Kingdom would have to be adjusted to take into account the absence of two leading designers early in the year, but that was all. The saddest part was that Emma's lovely Sturt Desert Pea vases would remain under wraps for another six months. What no-one outside the Works could have known was that final trials for the Australian flower had already been completed. Philip Allen's final choice had been for the 62/11 in an edition limited to one hundred pieces and the 226/7 in an edition limited to five hundred pieces. Both editions would carry a special Australia 2000 mark.

The bad news, as so often happens in life, came mixed with good news. Leading journalist, Ann Geneva, took a radical decision to abandon temporarily her contributions to the *Financial Times* and use the time made available to write a book on Moorcroft Enamels. The project was already under way when she first told Hugh of her decision. He was delighted. Originally American, Ann was now a citizen of the United Kingdom, and a total Moorcroft devotee. The Moorcroft chairman could think of no safer pair of hands to take on the task. The Hall family story would be investigated as thoroughly as the history of decorated enamels themselves. In so doing, a famous family business would be researched and documented before the truth about its development became buried under a heap of auction catalogue descriptions, anecdotal and edited fact, and the unresearched columns of commentators.

Ann's news reminded Hugh that Moorcroft Enamels also had to prepare itself for the millennium, in addition to Cobridge Stoneware and Moorcroft. The Design Studio had virtually completed its Moorcroft work. Much as Hugh had anticipated, Beverley Wilkes had responded positively to his hint that Meknes was capable of adaptation, while Shirley Hayes had simplified her work on Palmata. In its streamlined form, Hugh invited Shirley to design a few further trials for a possible range. Apart from fine tuning, the only items outstanding were the special pieces required for the pre-millennium Collectors' Christmas Weekend scheduled by Elise Adams to take place over the last weekend of November. What Hugh had not anticipated was that Phil Gibson had already moved forward with preparatory work for a new range tentatively called Rhododendron. As a design it had a vaguely 'traditional' look about it, but Phil was asked to continue notwithstanding.

In the interest of sound and sensitive management there was still the need to find out what collectors might like to see when the Moorcroft Enamels catalogue came off the press in January 2000. In part this could be deduced from the 1999 sales returns, in part from collectors' comments over the 1999 Open Weekend, where Elliot Hall's company was both fully and extraordinarily successfully represented, and in part from the enthusiasm with which the new Lilliputian Moorcroft shapes had been received by retailers' customers all over the world. Elliot Hall and the Moorcroft sales team would all be consulted about millennium designs for Moorcroft Enamels. This information had to be assessed and analysed before the Design Studio could move forward with its work.

Everyone felt that the pre-millennium Christmas Weekend needed a strong focal point to present to collectors, especially Moorcroft's newest main board appointee, Kim Thompson. It was one thing to say that pieces designed for the occasion would be the last of the old era, destined to join the ranks of Anemone Blue, Magnolia Ivory, Bramble, Violet and the rest to become part of Moorcroft's history. Kim wanted rather more than that, and as so often happens, fate intervened. Months earlier, Hugh had enjoyed one of his increasingly fascinating conversations with Walter Moorcroft, during which historical facts frequently fell into place, and where Walter's own huge and caring contribution to Moorcroft's art was often discussed. From these dialogues between the two men, new ideas had a habit of emerging.

Precisely who suggested that Walter should design a new piece as a dramatic prelude to the millennium is a matter for debate, but the result was a steady stream of trials of a remarkable design created in shades of blue, green, grey and white. Rock of Ages, Walter called it. Further enquiry established that the rocky seascape was Trearddur Bay on the island of Anglesey. Walter prepared the design for introduction on the 101/14, the 101/7, and a 15cm coaster. After more than twenty trials, he announced that Rock of Ages was ready for production, something not possible under Moorcroft's new design approval process. Hugh need not have worried. Rock of Ages was nodded through the first available design meeting on all three shapes.

It was largely because of the difficulty in slotting Rock of Ages into the Moorcroft production schedule that a decision was made to bring the design forward for the November celebrations. The 36cm vase would be an edition limited to fifty pieces and the 18cm vase an edition of one hundred pieces. The coaster would be a numbered edition, production of which would end on 31 December 1999. In this way, something prestigious would be available for collectors, indeed something so prestigious that Collectors' Christmas Weekend would take on a momentum all its own. At the same time, the new century and the new millennium would dawn with Moorcroft facing the world of the applied arts relying on its Design Studio alone. In so doing, it would become in full control of its own destiny.

FACING: *Herb Collection. Tallest vase 20cm (8").*

*Everglade Flamingos. Tallest vase 30cm (12").*

There were other signs that people were increasingly eager to see Moorcroft continue to look forwards rather than backwards. Outside the Moorcroft orbit, a decision had been taken by the charity that owned the building to renovate Burslem Old Town Hall as a substantial heritage project, backed with funds from the National Lottery. The Ceramica project was a major millennium showcase for the ceramics industry. Those who know the Potteries will recall that Burslem is at the far end of Nile Street, beyond Cobridge Stoneware, the Dudson distribution centre and the Royal Doulton factory.

The origin of the suggestion that Moorcroft should participate is unclear, but Mr John was asked to look after the company's interest. Several meetings took place before the Ceramica design team submitted their final text for the visitors' brochure to Mr John for approval. Realising that Hugh was keen to include Cobridge Stoneware in the Ceramica project as well as Moorcroft itself, Mr John passed on the final text for the Ceramica Visitors' Brochure to him for its accuracy to be checked. Why Mr John had taken this step was unclear, until Hugh read the text. It was a history of Moorcroft without a single reference whatsoever to the lifetime contribution of Walter to the company. Indeed it was difficult to establish from reading the text that Moorcroft still existed. It seemed that all those involved in the construction of the text felt there had to be a balance only between the past and the more recent past.

With Kim Thompson's help, Hugh re-wrote the text to incorporate Walter's achievements, introduced Cobridge Stoneware as a new company to Ceramica to make sure that all concerned knew that both Moorcroft and Cobridge Stoneware are both very much alive. In came references to their active Collectors' Clubs and the recent launch of Cobridge Stoneware as 'the new kid on the block' — Ceramica's words, not Hugh's! Suddenly the storyline came to life. A few days later Kim organised a meeting with the Ceramica architects to discuss layouts for both the Moorcroft and Cobridge Stoneware displays. The detail was important, but the message even more so. Ceramica was all about being alive, about making fine earthenware and china in the year 2000 and beyond. All the great Burslem names were there: Royal Doulton, H & R Johnson, Steelite, Dudson and Wade, to name but a few, but each offered only a line or two of their history and many paragraphs about the present and the future.

For some inexplicable reason, Hugh offered a sepia photograph of William Moorcroft to strengthen the graphics. 'No dead white flesh, please' was the architect's solemn response. Kim glared at the company Chairman, who felt embarrassed at making the offer in the first place. Ceramica was a showcase for living companies, not a shrine for dead men. In an effort to recover his lost ground, Hugh volunteered a fully-coloured, very much alive photograph of Walter for Ceramica's graphics, since the subject himself was very much alive and still designing. This raised smiles all around. Ceramica also commissioned a massive RM3 vase made with fibre glass and decorated with Rachel's Poppy design. Standing almost four metres high, the huge replica became a central feature of the Moorcroft stand. Other important keynotes were the first example of Nicola Slaney's Jerusalem vase and an eerily accurate life-size model of a Moorcroft tube-liner at work. Display layouts were agreed, and both Moorcroft and Cobridge Stoneware were put into a state of advanced readiness to meet the general public in Ceramica at the dawn of the millennium. With hindsight, it was just as well that Walter was written back into the Moorcroft story. In the Queen's birthday honours he was awarded an OBE!

As often happens in the world of the applied arts, the greatest struggle often becomes the greatest success. Whenever this happens the whole artistic process starts rolling like a snowball, gathering momentum and size as it moves

*Kapok Tree. Height 12cm (5").*

*Two of Cathedral's three panels. Height 40cm (16").*

downhill on its own. So it was with Nicola Slaney's Jerusalem vase, Phil Gibson's Everglade Flamingos and Herb Collection. Even Debbie Hancock's attractive Kapok Tree on the new 403/5 shape with its tumbling red flowers on a woodsmoke and golden brown ground slipped through almost unnoticed. Bombax Kelba had been identified as the Collectors' Day vase for the year 2000, and as such was destined to be sold at shops hosting Collectors' Days during the millennium year. All passed the early trial processes and on to full design approval without obstruction.

For collectors, the Herb Collection was something new. What Philip Gibson had designed was a collectable within a collectable: six vases each carrying a different pattern, each a different size and shape. With his Flamingos came a really novel combination of colour to dress the graceful and colourful birds in their natural habitat. Rhododendron was already trialled on six shapes, all of which eased their way through the September design meeting almost unnoticed and without correction, much to Phil's delight. With Meknes still on course for its planned design transformation and Palmata trials emerging weekly, the millennium offering from Moorcroft to the world was fast turning into an occasion without parallel.

There were whispers about, too. Rachel, already working on her Cathedral vase, had been seen drawing a range of ancient sailing ships. The senior designer's inspiration for Cathedral was her love of stained glass. The transfer of stained glass design styles into ceramic design was an extremely clever way to create images which were totally different to anything Moorcroft had ever done before. In much the same way as Nicola's Jerusalem design acknowledged the link between architecture and ceramic art, so Rachel's innovative approach linked the work of glassmakers to her own. The result was a totally fresh combination of ceramic images. Archangel Gabriel might just as well have featured in an altar window: the Garden of Eden was both subtle and suggestive at the same time while the flotilla of small boats struck a cord in Hugh's mind as soon as he saw it. What better than to let the boats spill out of the stained glass window on which they had been drawn and into a full Moorcroft range called Winds of Change? Rachel agreed and with her decision Hugh found not only the title to his new book but a design for the cover at the same time.

# TWENTY

# Sailing Overseas

Young and tough, Paul Blurton is the manager in charge of Moorcroft's accounts at National Westminster Bank. Paul represents a new breed of bank manager, trained in the art of financial prudence, supportive where justified and seemingly hard to please on problems created by financial carelessness or bad management. With the bank's help, the site for the new Macintyre works in Nile Street had been acquired in the summer of 1999. By the time the millennium dawned it would be time to take the vital decision on whether to proceed with the development of the site with the help of a large inner-city regeneration grant, or to defer the project and lose the grant. For Moorcroft the decision was finely balanced, but the company decided to proceed. This was done partly on the strength of potential Internet sales, partly on a determination to accelerate its export drive, partly on the continued growth in membership within the Collectors Club and most important of all, on the strength of its existing business. Taken together, these reasons made it possible for Paul Blurton to lodge a successful credit recommendation to the bank's credit committee. The bank's agreement to help finance the scheme enabled another Moorcroft dream to become a reality.

At the same time as these far-reaching strategic decisions were being made, Peter Hughes, sales director at Moorcroft for two years, resigned to pursue a career away from the company. In his place the board appointed the much-loved and hugely respected Alan Wright, a shareholder for many years and the man who, after his arrival in 1987, almost single-handedly increased Moorcroft sales to levels which ensured the company's survival following its two-year dance with death from 1984 to 1986. Before the new millennium was more than a few days old, Alan, together with Scotland's agent, Donald Reid, made a snap visit to the Atlanta, Georgia trade fair. Their subsequent report highlighted a huge potential demand for Moorcroft in the United States.

While Alan and Donald were away in Atlanta, Moorcroft focused its at-

FACING: *Winds of Change. Tallest vase 30cm (12").*

Simeon. Tallest vase 22 cm (9").

tention on the growing export potential for Moorcroft elsewhere in the world. By the way of encouragement, a letter came in from an international sales agent requesting a special limited edition for Brunei, some pieces from which were to be presented by the Sultan to twenty-seven heads of state including the President of the United States. The sting in the tail was a suggestion that the commission should be linked to a condition which credited Nicola Slaney's fine artwork to a Brunei resident and not Nicola. Hugh would have none of it and wrote to say so in uncompromising terms. For too long designers at Moorcroft had seen their credits occasionally stolen by those who had never designed anything in their lives. That unpleasant and misleading habit had been stamped out after 1997. As a result, those who were not designers but who liked having their photograph taken holding Moorcroft pottery in various poses were barred from doing so ever again. If the potential credit theft caused the design to die as a special Brunei commission, it would be a relatively simple manoeuvre to bring forward the design into the 2001 catalogue on the same 121/14 shape already selected by Nicola.

Exports would not benefit to the same extent if the commission failed, but collectors outside Brunei would have the opportunity to buy a superb limited edition design in 2001. Indeed, there was no reason why the edition should not be called 'Brunei'. Nicola's art work was too good to waste. The winds of change at Moorcroft had already blown away the false claims of human holograms asserting or pretending that other people's designs were their own. Design Studio members would keep all credits for their own work with each authorising the others to sign on their behalf whenever collectors requested. That had already been decided.

*Indian Paintbrush watercolour
by Philip Gibson*

Designer Philip Gibson had at various times spent many happy weeks climbing some of the toughest and most dangerous rock faces in the United States. With the sales team persistently enthusiastic about the warm reception for Moorcroft at the Atlanta giftware show, Phil set to work on a new design of his own. What emerged was Indian Paintbrush, the state flower of Wyoming. The watercolour was magnificent, featuring the hot desert mesas of the American West framed by one of the loveliest and most romantic of all flowers. For his first trial, Phil had used the 576/9 shape, but the plan was to bring forward a range of upwards of ten pieces. If there was time, Indian Paintbrush would first be offered in the United States at another Atlanta Gift Fair in July. Beyond that in February 2001 the design would appear at the International Spring Fair at Birmingham.

What particularly struck a cord with production director Keith Dawson was Phil's introduction of geometric hieroglyphics into Indian Paintbrush making it reminiscent of the famous and highly collectable Hopi Indian ceramic designs. Only the larger pieces in Phil's range carried the mesa images. The smaller pieces featured Indian Paintbrush flowers on their own. Keith's millennium holiday in America included a visit to the Hopi Indian reservation. A search for Indian Paintbrush flowers in the wild would add a fresh and colourful dimension to his holiday. For his own part, Hugh was mesmerised by the first prototype vase. Out of the base grew three Indian Paintbrush plants, initially hugging the contours of the vase before breaking out into a vibrant mass of reddish orange flower heads. In the centre, a warm sandy canyon and mesa landscape melt into the distance until it finally merges peacefully into the horizon. The use of a cool blue in the sky takes the heat out of the design, doubly so because the sky faded from blue to a subtle evening yellow with great effect.

*Simeon. Tallest vase 25 cm (10").*

With the American initiative well underway and Moorcroft's millennium exports on track to double by the company's year end, the first of Paul Blurton's loan support criteria was well on the way to fulfilment. The more speculative Internet drive would follow. Hugh had never been over-excited about the Internet. The bottom line was that Moorcroft could claim credit for all of its pottery made and sold via the Internet in the past, present and future.

Almost immediately the decision to proceed with a second new factory in

*Simeon charger. Diameter 35cm (14").*

Nile Street had been taken, another curious problem raised its head. It would take more than a year to complete the construction of the Macintyre works at the rear of the site and a further year to complete phase II at the front of the site. As Maureen was quick to point out, the tube-liners and decorators who were also mothers of children in the Moorcroft nursery would soon have to look for another nursery to care for their two year old toddlers. They were not in a position to wait while Moorcroft got its act together. Something had to be done, Keith told the board. The company had recently acquired a house in Walley Place adjacent to the Cobridge Stoneware factory, but to convert it into a nursery would cost four times the original price paid for the house itself. For a building which had only a two-year lifespan as a temporary nursery, expenditure of that kind could not be justified.

The mothers' disappointment was obvious, and they offered Moorcroft a solution of their own. Rachel, as senior designer and a nursery mother herself, had been asked by the other nursery mothers to design a special vase in her own time. She agreed. In turn, the tube-liners and decorators with babies in the nursery also agreed among themselves to complete a special limited edition for collectors to be sold in the Moorcroft factory shop. The work would be unpaid and undertaken in their own time. To keep Paul Blurton and his colleagues at NatWest happy, Hugh and Maureen personally guaranteed a loan of the amount required to complete the conversion. With the arrival of a temporary planning permission for nursery use, the contractors moved on site shortly before Christmas. From Rachel came Baby Blue Eyes, delicately presented on the 99/8 shape. The design carried with it an emotional charge so strong that anyone on the design committee speaking against it ran a severe risk of being seen as a latter-day Ebenezer Scrooge!

*Baby Blue Eyes.*
*Height 20 cm (8").*

Before the end of November, Philip Gibson had finished work on his deceptively simple Rhododendron design. Both design and colours had a vaguely 'old Moorcroft' feel about them. The dark blue base of each piece shaded to a really attractive cream at the rim and the flowers were a vibrant red. More interesting still were the lamps, which carried a slightly simplified design, albeit with the same colour combination. No shapes used for lamps were duplicated elsewhere in the Rhododendron range. This fact on its own added a novel feature to an otherwise comfortable approach to Moorcroft creativity.

Moorcroft's agent in Scotland, Donald Reid, gave a whoop of delight as soon as he set eyes on Rhododendron. For decades the Scots have been perceptive and careful collectors, and always good friends of Moorcroft through good times and bad. In Donald's view the Scots were likely to move on Rhododendron in a big way. The shrub is a familiar sight in many Scottish gardens, but for Donald the design meant much more than that. The colours were alive and the images moved around each piece with a strength that made them totally irresistible. Donald was a good Scot, an eternal and cheerful optimist, a brilliant salesperson and a colourful member of the Moorcroft corporate family. More significantly, when Donald offered an opinion on the Scots, it was usually accurate and to the point.

*Shirley Hayes*

Hugh had also been looking hard at Phil's Rhododendron design, but with a totally different thought in his mind. A year or so earlier, a Rhododendron vase had emerged at Open Weekend; for two different designs to carry the same name was a potential source of confusion. With one eye on Anna, Nicola Slaney's new lily design, another possible name for Rhododendron emerged from the darker recesses of Hugh's mind. His idea had a biblical ring about it. The year 2000 was, after all, a landmark in the Christian calendar. Tentatively Maureen was sounded out, as was Phil himself. Both agreed, and overnight Rhododendron became Simeon. It remained to see which collector would be the first to come forward with the correct reason for the change of name.

Autumn had more surprises in store for the overworked Moorcroft team producing tube-lining and painting trials than the arrival of Simeon, with or without its new name. Nicola's Fruit Garden range was already complete with its mix of luscious strawberries and delicate blossom clinging to a plant which grew organically from the base of each piece in a way that would have forced William Morris to turn his head. On that mysterious list which Hugh carried around permanently in his head, Fruit Garden had the word 'delivered' written alongside the design. The surprise that threw him completely off balance was the arrival of a letter from a designer called Sian Leeper. Sian had

FACING: *Palmata. Tallest vase 22cm (9").*

first joined Moorcroft in 1992 following an introduction from the design team in charge at the time, and in less than a year she had learned both how to tube-line and to paint in the Moorcroft idiom as successfully as if she had worked at the two great skills all her life.

At the end of 1992, Moorcroft's third full-time designer had left the company. Sadly for Moorcroft, Sian left at the same time. She worked for Moorcroft's former design team for three years afterwards, and then on and off over the ensuing years. After a spell in the United States, Sian had decided to take a long hard look at her life, and with commendable resilience wrote to Hugh to ask if there were any vacancies in the Moorcroft Design Studio. As it happened, there was one remaining place to be filled, but only one. Shortly after two successful interviews, each backed with an impressive design portfolio which included polar bears, not to mention a large assortment of other animals, birds and landscapes, Sian arrived at Moorcroft. Not only did she have a good design degree to back her claim, but also the additional bonus that her tube-lining and painting skills had become even better than they had been in 1992.

With her dual skills, Sian joined Nicola Slaney as the only member of the Design Studio with the distinction of being a designer, tube-liner and painter all in one. Another gift Sian brought with her to Moorcroft was her ability to train both tube-liners and painters, something she had undertaken successfully for her previous employers. As a result she would be available to join Sue Fairhead, Gwyneth Hibbitt and Marj Hill in the new Nile Street training school. All that was for the future. To serve the present, Sian set to work as a designer. Hard work and total commitment ensured that her colourful frogs appeared in time for the Moorcroft Collectors Club Christmas party. No sooner had they jumped into view than a stunning pictorial design emerged from the glost kiln showing a

*Geneva. Tallest vase 20 cm (8").*

FACING: *Palmata. Tallest vase 20 cm (8").*

*Sian Leeper and her Pride of Lions ginger jar. Height 15 cm (6").*

pride of lions set off to perfection on the African plains. Not surprisingly, the ginger jar carrying the design was christened Pride of Lions.

Simultaneously, around the corner at Cobridge Stoneware, sea eagles began to soar above lakes, mountains and forests on a number of pieces. Sian's work had all the qualities necessary to strengthen the stoneware pottery's presentation at the millennium. Nor had Elliot Hall at Worcester been forgotten. For Moorcroft Enamels, Sian designed and delivered a limited edition Leopard vase as well as some Moorcroft Polar Bears in miniature. Her work, like that of her colleagues in the Design Studio, was young, fresh and innovative, and before Moorcroft closed down for the Christmas holiday, retailers were telephoning to secure early examples of Sian's work for the year 2000.

A third design meeting saw Shirley Hayes' Palmata design approved on eight shapes plus two lamps. The rich red flowerheads were shown off to maximum design advantage through the subtle use of a dark woodsmoke ground fading almost to black both at the rim and the base of each piece. As a collectors range, Palmata was full of indefinable promise. It was, Hugh confided to his wife, the kind of design he would have gone for in a big way in his collecting years. There was something timeless about Palmata, and whether it was long-lived or short-lived as a design, it had all the ingredients of a real collectors' favourite.

At the same meeting which saw Palmata pass through the approval process, Phil's Gentian design suffered a minor reverse. Those present decided that as a design it was excellent, but both the line work and the colours were so intricate that a premium price would be inevitable. To ease the strain on collectors' credit cards, out of the original six pieces submitted only the 393/4 and 122/8 were approved for production. The trials for the rejected shapes were released over the 1999 Collectors Christmas weekend at the end of November where they were joined by a superb collection specially created by Design Studio members for the occasion. Snowflakes from heaven, Hugh thought to himself. Phil's contribution was a Peony jug set against a blue/green ground with delicate but full pink flowers, and leaves which faded from almost moss green to brown at the tips. The committee of the British Ceramic Confederation was so taken by the Peony design that they commissioned two huge planters to sit either side of the fireplace in their refurbished club lounge. Meanwhile Shirley Hayes, perhaps the most reticent member of the Design Studio, had not forgotten Moorcroft collectors. Her Astrantia vases came in a number of deceptively simple colourways. Interestingly, the design was seen by many to have all the qualities of old Moorcroft Florianware, and as if to confirm that conclusion, leading journalist, Ann Geneva, actually repeated the comment in a subsequent edition of the Moorcroft Newsletter.

Dawn and dusk pieces, both made to the same design, followed the success of Angela Davenport's Samburu Giraffes several months earlier, but this time the initiative originated from the ever-active Debbie Hancock. Called simply 'Quayside', and featuring sailing boats, waterside cottages and railings all set against a backcloth of distant hills, the vases had an almost dream-like quality about them. Indeed, for Hugh, Quayside was one of the most restful designs to come out of Moorcroft since Rachel Bishop's much-loved Lamia. Also demonstrating the alternative colourway technique to great effect, Angela Davenport took the versatile Bougainvillea shrub to work up into a design. Below its climbing flowers and leaves she introduced a stylised lattice wall to enhance the suggestion of Mediterranean warmth and tranquillity.

As much for fun as for art, the versatile Beverley Wilkes cleverly adapted a familiar Moorcroft shape to create a more than realistic miniature bottle oven. After animated discussion at a design meeting it was decided that Beverley's bottle oven would be produced in an edition limited to one hundred pieces. More surprisingly, and also with a twist of humour, Okra Glass designer, Sarah Cowan, introduced herself to Moorcroft collectors with Wisdom the Owl on the ever-popular 7/7 shape in an edition limited to fifty pieces. Sarah, better known as a master glassmaker in the complex world of the applied arts, decided to set to work on a Moorcroft design more out of a sense of occasion than duty. As an Okra Glass designer she is automatically a member of the Moorcroft Design Studio. So is her colleague and mentor at Okra, Richard Golding. Wisdom the Owl flew, as they say, and

*Penstemon. Height 30 cm (12").*

*Quayside. Height 25 cm (10").*

before the 1999 November Weekend closed, not a single piece remained perched on the shelves in the factory shop.

Emma Bossons, always careful and totally in control of the art of simplicity, decided to use the textured clover flower as her design theme. On the tiny 35/3 shape, she wove together a lifelike clover flower in shades of purple and pink set against a soft blue ground fading in some cases to cream. Her friend and fellow designer, Nicola Slaney, offered Penstemon on the impressive 80/12 shape with maroon flowers winding round the base of the vase leaving buds and leaves to cling delicately to its fine neck. Using a similar colour palette, Nicola also designed a six inch vase on the 869 shape with a blue base which faded gently into a rich cream at the rim. Called appropriately 'November', collectors showed their approval by purchasing all thirty pieces put out for sale before the weekend closed.

Not one to let her colleagues down, Jeanne McDougall took the tough route to success by designing both Spring Flora and Autumn Hedgerow to a small four inch vase. It is considerably more difficult to design successfully to a small shape than to a large one, but for those good enough to succeed, the reward is that of high perceived value in the eyes of a collector. Flowing colours in Jeanne's favourite pinks and blues made both designs irresistible, so much so that Hugh succumbed to the two of them only to find that his wife, Maureen had done likewise!

Tired Moorcroft staff admitted to feeling a twinge of sadness as the last collector left for home and Sian Leeper's colourful Frogs hopped off into the darkness protected by generous portions of bubblewrap. Well over two thousand mince pieces had been consumed, all washed down with more than a hundred litres of mulled wine. Whichever way you measured it, the November weekend had been a great success. Everyone had enjoyed themselves, but the time had come for the world of reality to reassert itself. Phil's Gentian design on the 122/8 and 393/4 shapes were both approved the very next day for the millennium catalogue, the former as an edition limited to five hundred pieces and the latter to three hundred. Phil was delighted, doubly so because

TOP LEFT: *Bougainvillea (rear) Spring Flora (front left) and Autumn Hedgerow (centre front). Height of tall vases 15 cm (6").*
TOP RIGHT: *Astrantia. Height 20 cm (8").*
BELOW LEFT: *Clockwise Peony Jug; Frogs; Clover (2); November. Height of jug 17 cm (7")*
BELOW RIGHT: *Bottle Oven (left); Wisdom (right). Tall vase 17 cm (8").*

every one of his Gentian trials had been snapped up by collectors well before the close of the November weekend, with many collectors still asking whether any more existed. The millennium dawn was now little more than a month away, and the time had come to put the final arrangements in place.

At Moorcroft, the process of learning delivers harsh lessons almost daily. Corporate man, displaying one of his more ignorant features, will occasionally attempt to brand a design like Gentian as 'not commercial'. In the language of corporate man, this means 'too expensive'. Fortunately, in the world of the applied arts, the phrase 'not commercial' or 'too expensive' can be justified only when the design itself is of poor quality. If a design is of excellent quality, that quality will always carry a fair price. To make something 'cheaply' means precisely that. Collectors instinctively recognise the ingredients of something cheap. In the case of Moorcroft, poor quality design would lead to bankruptcy. High quality design and artistry carry all costs, as well as the maker's profit. Before the catalogues were printed, Phil's Gentian pieces changed their name to Geneva. Although they were not to know it at the time, the 'quality' brigade were soon to have the satisfaction of watching the 'not commercial' brigade grind their teeth. Under its new name of Geneva, both gentian limited edition designs sold out before the new millennium was six weeks old!

In the life of an art pottery, decisions are made from time to time with the best of intentions only to be overturned later for the best of reasons. One such case was a decision that there should be no exclusive limited editions for British retailers during the year 2000. What the Moorcroft board had overlooked was that the year 2000 included Liberty's '125 Birthday' as the store called it. In came Rachel's Cymric Dream. Also on Moorcroft's list of decisions for the millennium was a consensus for an exclusive limited edition with all proceeds of sale passing to a chosen charity.

At the time no decision had been taken on the identity of the charity, but as happens occasionally that particular question delivered its own answer. For some time Hugh had been a trustee of a national charity called the Low Pay Unit dedicated to eliminating poverty, discrimination and disadvantage in all their insidious forms in the United Kingdom. The chairman, Chris Pond MP, had run the charity successfully for more than twenty years before his election to Parliament; but at the end of 1999 he became obliged to resign as chairman on constitutional grounds when the Government appointed him a Treasury Minister. Hugh was elected chairman of the Low Pay Unit in his place. As a consequence, and at Hugh's request, the charity was nominated to be the beneficiary Moorcroft's millennium gift.

Once again it was Emma Bossons who came up with an apt design theme. On the timeless 32/5 shape, she drew some simple lilies of the valley. The white flowers had stalks lightly tube-lined in green. Each plant carried moderately dark green leaves, but it was the ground colour of the vase which made the collector in Hugh tingle all over. Black at the rim, the colour faded to orange and then red before reverting to black at the base. There was little Hugh could say, other than ask why lilies of the valley had provided Emma with her inspiration for the Low Pay Unit vase. Once again Hugh saw that fleeting smile and the distant twinkle in the designer's eyes. In her book, The Complete Language of Flowers, author Sheila Pickles points out that lilies of the valley symbolise 'the return of happiness'. From that short phrase, Emma took her inspiration. Now it was Hugh's turn to smile. Inside he felt more at ease, more happy than he had ever felt since he had joined Moorcroft full time. The dark days of 1997 had gone. For Hugh the millennium would deliver a new dawn. His thanks to Emma, both for Moorcroft and the Low Pay Unit, were more sincere than anyone would ever know.

*Lily of the Valley. Height 12cm (5″).*

# TWENTY ONE

# Millennium Showcase

Back in the summer of 1998, the BBC's magazine *Homes and Antiques* had been robust in their acknowledgement of the significance of Cobridge Stoneware's rediscovery of the high-fired flambé techniques of William Howson Taylor at Ruskin Pottery. *Collect-It!* magazine had done likewise. For Hugh, an approach from Gwyn Jones, the magazine's editor-in-chief, to discuss a new publishing venture came as no surprise. Gwyn was a good business innovator, an excellent television presenter and a writer who understood the problems and pleasures of the applied arts.

What Gwyn wanted was a special and exclusive limited edition to sell from the pages of her new publication *Antiques Lifestyle*. The greatest difficulty was a requirement for design approval well in advance of Christmas 1999, with delivery to follow early in the year 2000. Moorcroft agreed, despite the extra burden on its tube-liners, decorators and designer, Philip Gibson. What emerged from the glost kiln was a superb aquilegia jug, around which the elegant purple and pink flowers hung as gracefully as if they were actually clinging to the contours of the piece. Coming in a modest limited edition of 250, the jugs sold out before the millennium had even arrived. For perceptive collectors, Purple Aquilegia offered very good value.

Beverley Wilkes' impact on the millennium catalogue turned out to be far more significant than the vase Kerala on its own might have suggested. The designer had not forgotten the less than subtle hint whispered in her ear earlier in the year. What she produced for a startled Hugh to look at was a total transformation of her Meknes design. The foreground had become more formal with a dramatic black and white chequer-board effect, very much in the Arab style. The landscape retained its desert images much as it had done on both Meknes itself and the experimental Meknes at Night. It was, however, the dramatic use of much stronger architectural features that turned the design into something very

FACING: *Jumeirah. Tallest vase* 35cm. (14″).

special indeed. Bev sat looking at Hugh intensely. She knew that her work had provoked a strong and positive reaction.

His smile must have spoken volumes. For a man who had both lived and worked in the Middle East and who counted many senior Arab figures as his personal friends, the design was perfect. Its passage through the design meeting created a ripple of excitement, and the range was approved on nine shapes. Within days of the last trial, retailers were lining up to take some significant pieces of Jumeirah into their stores. Collectors' Club Secretary, Elise Adams, provided the name, borrowed from the desert town in the Gulf state of Dubai.

Even as the final designs slipped unobtrusively into place, Hugh started to assess the size of the task ahead. Never before in the whole of its hundred and three year history had Moorcroft produced so many new designs at one time. Once the decision had been taken to sever all Moorcroft's links with the previous century, some of the most powerful emotions Hugh had ever experienced in his working life surged one way and another. In place of Moorcroft's abandoned past would be no fewer than thirteen new ranges or collections and an unprecedented seven limited editions. If you count Rachel's superb Cymric Dream design for Liberty, Debbie Hancock's Spirit of the Lakes created to celebrate the centenary of Keswick retailers Treeby & Bolton, the Low Pay Unit's Lily of the Valley and Baby Blue Eyes itself, the total number of special editions becomes eleven. The surge of emotion was all about an uncharted future, a future vested in youth, in a new generation and a new millennium. What was needed was a fitting showcase to introduce the new work to the media and Moorcroft retailers alike.

On Armistice Day, Hugh found himself sitting with a committee headed by Susan Lambert at the Victoria and Albert Museum. What the V&A wanted from Moorcroft was a millennium lecture on the ceramics industry in Britain from the Moorcroft Chairman. What the Moorcroft Chairman wanted for Moorcroft was the use of the William Morris room in the museum as showcase for its millennium presentation. And so it occured. On 14 December the Moorcroft millennium pots met both the media and a representative sample of quality retailers at one and the same time. To add to the importance of the occasion, the entire Design Studio turned out to meet their public. Within days, BBC television cameras were filming at the Works, Jerusalem featured on London Weekend Television, and the Moorcroft designers generally found themselves the centre of attention from virtually every journalist, editor and producer involved in the applied arts.

Just minutes before the start of the Moorcroft showcase at the V&A the William Morris room was empty. The next, it was full to capacity. Hugh allowed himself the luxury of standing back to watch. For a fleeting moment, he felt old, isolated and alone, but it soon passed. The tasks he originally set himself at Moorcroft were complete, while in front of him the art pottery's millennium presentation was being admired by all who came to look. The setting was perfect. The room's wonderful wall fabrics and artistry, all made by William Morris and his team, formed the perfect backcloth to the greatest display of contemporary Moorcroft ever. In the centre of it all, colourful and proud, stood Jerusalem, almost melting into Morris' setting. Standing next to Jerusalem, its creator Nicola Slaney was trying to answer volley after volley of questions from excited press and retailer representatives. She deserved the accolades, all of them. Rachel was there too, talking to a leading magazine editor about Cathedral, Winds of Change and Gypsy. Already part of the Moorcroft legend, she was the designer who took Moorcroft's art over the bridge from one century to the next, from one millennium to another. Clearly happy at the reac-

*Aquilegia jug.*
*Height 24cm. (9¹⁄₂″).*

tion to her work, Moorcroft's senior designer had once again delivered quality to the task to which she may as well have been born.

Both the Moorcroft name and its art were now bigger than any single player. No longer could pride or personal ambition hold or control Moorcroft to suit the purposes of a particular person. As a result, Moorcroft was more secure. Gone was the reliance on a single heartbeat or perhaps two to survive. Its brilliant colours and eternal quality had become synonymous with the Moorcroft name, and as such the company was ready to grow and blossom within the complex world of the applied arts.

At its heart, Moorcroft needs love to move it forward, passion to make it work and commitment verging on obsession to make it succeed. Each person working for the company at the dawn of the millennium had his or her own part to play, and each understood how vital it was to give rather than take. To drain Moorcroft of love, of passion and of giving is the only sure way to destroy it. If those creating its art succeed, there will be songs in their hearts and a lightness of step as they come to work each day. To love is to give, and to share is to enjoy. Without giving there is no love and without love there is nothing to share. Those who cannot subscribe to this simple truth have no purpose to fulfil at Moorcroft, nor will they ever understand what it is about. Those very real people living in the city of Stoke on Trent who together made Moorcroft what it was in the past and make it what it is today have a pride in what they do, an openness in the way they work. Today, through profit-sharing, through pension and mutual reliance, each shares in the success of the company to which they have committed their lives.

With these thoughts rushing through his mind, Hugh found himself smiling. At the Works there was laughter and happiness, a friendship between people who live and work each day together in a common purpose. Deep inside Moorcroft there burns a great light which radiates warmth and security over all those it touches. It is that same warmth that collectors experience whenever they visit the Works, and which pulls them back time and time again. In some inexplicable way, they too feel part of the Moorcroft story – as indeed they are.

The years leading up to the millennium had turned out to be no more than a

prologue to a new age, the herald of a new order deriving its strength from love of a common purpose and loyalty among people, one to another, rather than dependence or subservience. Two thousand years ago a remarkable man tramped the rough hills of Palestine, a man who spoke of love, of equality and of sharing. What better way to greet the dawn of the new millennium than to honour the memory of that man and some of the philosophies he taught so many of us to understand.

*Spirit of the Lakes for Keswick retailers, Treeby and Bolton, to celebrate their centenary. Height 12 cm (5").*

Design Studio 2000

Photograph courtesy of Neil Brightmore Studios

# Moorcroft Marks

## TUBE-LINERS' MARKS

| | | | |
|---|---|---|---|
| Alicia Amison<br>1998 – Present | | Joyce Keeling<br>1993 – Present | |
| Janine Barrett<br>1999 – Present | | Louise Llewellyn<br>1998 – Present | |
| Alison Benson-Neale<br>1989 – Present | | Clare Lowe<br>1999 – Present | |
| Tonia Billings<br>1999 – Present | | Ruth Luby<br>1998 – Present | |
| Amanda Bourne<br>1994 – Present | | Kerry Edgerton (Marshall)<br>1997 – Present | |
| Julie-Anne Bowen<br>1998 – Present | | Lesley Myatt<br>1998 – Present | |
| Kelvin Dean<br>1996 – Present | | Sarah Pendlebury<br>1997 - Present | |
| Gillian Edge Powell<br>1998 – Present | | Marie Penkethman<br>1990 – Present | |
| Sue Griffin<br>1996 – Present | | Karen Potts<br>1989 – Present | |
| Hayley Grocott Smith<br>1995 – Present | | Catherine Smith<br>1992 – Present | |
| Julie Harrison<br>1993 – Present | | Valerie Smith<br>1997 – 1999 (Dcd) | |
| Sandra Hartshorne<br>1998 – Present | | Clare Sneyd<br>1996 – Present | |
| Caroline Hulme<br>1996 – Present | | Janette Sneyd<br>2000 – Present | |
| Gillian Leese (Johnson)<br>1985 – Present | | Stephanie Snow<br>1998 – Present | |
| Julie Johnson<br>1998 – Present | | Vicky Thorley<br>1998 – Present | |
| Paula Jones<br>1998 – Present | | Leanne Turner<br>1998 – 1999 | |
| Kath Keeling<br>1998 – Present | | Tracy Weston<br>1999 – Present | |
| | | Ailie Woodhead-Coates<br>1987 – Present | |

## PAINTERS' MARKS

| | | | | |
|---|---|---|---|---|
| Sharon Austin 1987 – Present | | Sylvia Evans 1991 – Present | |
| Amanda Baggley 1995 – Present | | Sue Fairhead 1998 – Present | |
| Amanda Baker 1996 – Present | | Victoria Ford 1999 – Present | |
| Sue Barnsley 1995 – Present | | Paula Gaitley 1990 – Present | |
| Chris Bell 1998 – Present | | Donna Gerrard 1999 – Present | |
| Heather Bettany 1998 – Present | | Sue Gibbs 1984 – Present | |
| Laura Blight 1998 – Present | | Dawn Hall 1998 – Present | |
| Emma Bossons 1996 – Present | | Debbie Hancock 1992 – Present | |
| Amanda Bourne 1997 – Present | | Jayne Hancock 1987 – Present | |
| Mandy Breeze 1987 – 1998 | | Peter Harrison 1998 – Present | |
| Jim Carroll 1999 – Present | | Shirley Hayes 1992 – Present | |
| Naomi Carroll 1999 – Present | | Laura Hewitt 1998 – Present | |
| Helen Dale 1999 – Present | | Gwyneth Hibbitt 1973 – Present | |
| Angela Davenport 1995 – Present | | Paul Hilditch 1999 – Present | |
| Julie Dolan 1984 – Present | | Marjorie Hill 1987 – Present | |
| Alison Edwards 1997 – Present | | Kerry Hopkinson 1998 – Present | |
| Julie Edwards 1999 – Present | | Elizabeth Hughes 1997 – Present | |
| Louise Edwards 1999 – Present | | Lorraine Knowles 1997 – Present | |
| Mary Etheridge 1987 – Present | | Jennifer Kowalkowski 1989 – Present | |

| | | | |
|---|---|---|---|
| Sian Leeper<br>1999 – Present | *Sian* | Claire Shelley<br>1999 – Present | Ⓢ |
| Vicky Lovatt<br>1999 – Present | *Vh* | Glynn Simpson<br>1999 – Present | *GS* |
| Patricia May<br>1998 – Present | *PM* | Nicola Slaney<br>1997 – Present | *NS* |
| Karen Mellor<br>1995 – Present | *KM* | Deborah Smith<br>1999 – Present | *DS* |
| Paula Mellor<br>1999 – Present | *PM* | Hayley Smith<br>1988 – Present | *HS* |
| Hayley Moore<br>1987 – Present | *HM* | Maggie Thompson<br>1991 – Present | *Mag* |
| Jackie Moores<br>1998 – Present | *JM* | Wendy Thorne (Mason)<br>1979 – Present | *W* |
| Joanne Morton<br>1994 – Present | *JM* | Christina Turnock<br>1998 – Present | *CRL* |
| Barbara Mountford<br>1987 – Present | *BM* | Karen Walker<br>1998 – Present | *KW* |
| Joanne Mountford<br>1993 – Present | *JM* | Joanne Walton<br>1999 – Present | *JLW* |
| Lisa Phillips<br>1991 – Present | *L* | Chris Walton<br>1998 – Present | *cw* |
| Sue Pointon<br>1988 – Present | *SP* | Joanne White<br>1997 – Present | *JW* |
| Johann Price<br>1998 – 1999 | *JP* | Beverley Wilkes<br>1989 – Present | *BW* |
| Carolyn Pugh<br>1997 – Present | *Cp* | Mandy Wood<br>1994 – Present | *W* |
| Emma Rafferty<br>1994 – Present | *ER* | Nicola Woodward<br>1999 – Present | *NW* |
| Mandy Rashford-Jones<br>1999 – Present | *MRJ* | Joanne Wootton<br>1999 – Present | *Jo* |
| Jackie Rowe<br>1992 – Present | *JR* | Linda Worthington<br>1999 – Present | *LW* |

## RETAILER AND DISTRIBUTOR MARKS 1997–2000

Underwood: made exclusively for James Macintyre & Co Ltd in a limited edition of 350 pieces.

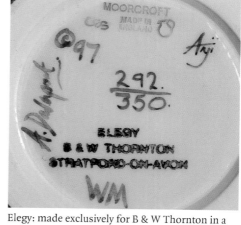

Elegy: made exclusively for B & W Thornton in a limited edition of 350 vases.

Castle Garden: made exclusively for Talents of Windsor in a limited edition of 500 pieces.

Sturt Desert Pea design made as a 27cm (11") vase and a 18cm (7") vase in an edition of 100 and 500 respectively for Moorcroft Australia Pty, with a special distributor's mark.

Hawthorn: made exclusively for Liberty in a limited edition of 400 pieces.

Spirit of the Lakes: made exclusively to commemorate the centenary of Keswick retailers, Treeby & Bolton. A limited edition of 250 pieces.

## YEAR STAMPS 1997 – 2000

| | | | | | |
|---|---|---|---|---|---|
| 1997 | H | Centenary Mark (H & C for Roman hundred) | 1999 | (jug symbol) | Jug |
| 1998 | (iron symbol) | Iron | 2000 | (key symbol) | Key |

## SPECIAL MARKS

Limited edition mark.

A Trial and Dated mark.

Moorcroft Design Studio symbol. First used in 1999.

From 2000 onwards the impressed mark 'Moorcroft/ Made in / England', in use since the First World War, was changed to 'Moorcroft / Stoke on Trent / England'.

A numbered edition mark.

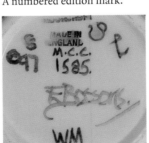

M.C.C. identifies a piece designed exclusively for the Moorcroft Collectors' Club or for Moorcroft Collectors' Club Open Weekends, in both May and November.

Training mark – identified by the 'T' mark. Note also the © copyright mark, now on every piece produced.

# INDEX

## References to illustrations in bold